COLLECTOR'S VALUE GUIDE

BOYDS BEARS & FRIENDS ™

The Bearstone Collection®
The Folkstone Collection®
The Dollstone Collection™
The Shoe Box Bears™
DeskAnimals™

Secondary Market Price Guide
& Collector Handbook

FOURTH EDITION

BOYDS BEARS & FRIENDS ™

Front cover: "Gary, Tina, Matt & Bailey . . . From Our Home To Yours," *The Bearstone Collection.*

Back cover (left to right): "Bumble B. Bee . . . Sweeter Than Honey," *The Bearstone Collection*; "Shannon & Wilson . . . Wait'n For Grandma," *The Dollstone Collection*; "Ms. Fries . . . Guardian Angel Of Waitresses," *The Folkstone Collection*; "Arnold P. Bomber . . . The Duffer," *The Bearstone Collection.*

Managing Editor:	Jeff Mahony		Art Director:	Joe T. Nguyen
Associate Editors:	Melissa A. Bennett		Production Supervisor:	Scott Sierakowski
	Jan Cronan		Graphic Designers:	Lance Doyle
	Gia C. Manalio			Kimberly Eastman
	Paula Stuckart			Ryan Falis
Contributing Editor:	Mike Micciulla			Jason C. Jasch
Editorial Assistants:	Jennifer Filipek			David S. Maloney
	Nicole LeGard Lenderking			David Ten Eyck
	Ren Messina			
	Joan C. Wheal			
Research Assistants:	Priscilla Berthiaume			
	Beth Hackett			
	Steven Shinkaruk			

ISBN 1-888914-47-5

CHECKERBEE™ and COLLECTOR'S VALUE GUIDE™ are trademarks of CheckerBee, Inc.

CheckerBee **PUBLISHING**

(formerly Collectors' Publishing)
306 Industrial Park Road • Middletown, CT 06457

www.collectorbee.com

TABLE OF CONTENTS

Introducing The Collector's Value Guide™ 5

Overview – Boyds Resin Figurines 6

Sneak Peek At Boyds Plush Animals 11

Inside The Wacky World Of Boyds.............. 14

Spotlight On Gary Lowenthal 17

What's New For Boyds Resin Figurines 23

Collector's Club News 36

Future Retirements 38

Bearstone Top Ten 41

Folkstone Top Five 44

Dollstone Top Five 45

How To Use Your Collector's Value Guide™ 46

Value Guide – Boyds Bears & Friends™ 47

THE BEARSTONE COLLECTION® 47

General Figurines.................................. 47

Holiday Pageant Series 73

Noah's Pageant Series........................ 77

Clocks 78

Frames 78

Musicals 79

Ornaments.................................. 80

Plaques 85

Sconces 86

Votive Holders 86

Waterglobes................................ 89

San Francisco Music Boxes 90

Bearwear Pins.............................. 96

THE FOLKSTONE COLLECTION® 101

General Figurines 101

Carvers Choice 122

Santa & Friends............................ 125

TABLE OF CONTENTS

The Wee Folkstones 126
Ribbit & Co.................................. 132
Frames 135
Musicals 136
Ornaments 136
Sconces...................................... 142
Votive Holders................................ 142
Waterglobes 143
Folkwear Pins 144

THE DOLLSTONE COLLECTION™ 148
General Figurines............................. 148
Frames 158
Musicals 159
Ornaments 159
Porcelain Dolls 160
Votive Holders 163
Waterglobes 164
San Francisco Music Boxes 164

THE SHOE BOX BEARS™ 165

DESK ANIMALS™ 168

COLLECTOR'S CLUB 171

Future Releases 175
Total Value Of My Collection.................... 178
Secondary Market Overview 181
Variations.................................... 186
Insuring Your Collection 192
Production And Pricing 193
Glossary 194
Bearfinder – Numerical Index 196
Bearfinder – Alphabetical Index 200

INTRODUCING THE COLLECTOR'S VALUE GUIDE™

$\mathscr{F}$or the first time ever, here is a Collector's Value Guide™ dedicated *exclusively* to the delightfully offbeat and extremely popular resin characters of The Boyds Collection Ltd.

EVERYTHING ABOUT THE "BEAN" IN THE BEAR BIZ

First, you will explore the history of Boyds resin figurines and be introduced to Gary Lowenthal, the creative seed behind the Boyds family tree. Next, you will climb from branch to branch, exploring each collection: The Bearstone Collection, The Folkstone Collection, The Dollstone Collection, The Shoe Box Bears and DeskAnimals. After a quick look at Boyds plush animals, you will swing through insightful, and often hilarious, bits of Boyds trivia. And you won't want to miss the spotlight on the "Head Bean Hisself!"

Then it's on to the exciting news of 1999! There you'll discover this season's introductions, future retirements and the most valuable members of each collection. Next explore the new, improved Value Guide section, featuring larger-than-ever color photos and comprehensive, up-to-date information, including secondary market values.

AND MORE!?!...

Also packed into this valuable guide are features on variations, information on insurance coverage, a look at the secondary market and a glossary of the language native to the land of The Boyds Collection Ltd. And so much more!

*W*here was The Boyds Collection Ltd. born? Why, in Boyds, Maryland of course! Gary M. Lowenthal, the president and chief designer of all things Boyds, found himself in this rural Maryland community after his "big-city" upbringing on Manhattan Island, a higher educational hiatus in upstate New York and a subsequent Peace Corps stint in the Fiji Islands. Lowenthal then spent seven years at Bloomingdales in New York City where he learned the fine art of purchasing, design and merchandising. Unsatisfied with the concrete jungle of city life, Lowenthal took his family and moved south to Maryland, to follow his dreams of opening a small antiques shop. Working out of a historic farmhouse, Lowenthal began what today is known as The Boyds Collection Ltd. with a line of hand-carved duck decoys and some ceramic homes fit for gnomes.

Once again in 1987, Lowenthal packed up the family and headed for Gettysburg, Pennsylvania. This quirky entrepreneur then took the next logical ("Head Bean" logic, that is) step and began a line of plush animals. Enjoying some success with these stuffed and furry critters, the energetic "Head Bean Hisself" was inspired to

The Boyds Collection

The Bearstone Collection

The Folkstone Collection

The Dollstone Collection

The Shoe Box Bears

Desk Animals

replicate the plush bears and add some friends into a new line of resin figurines. The Bearstone Collection was introduced in 1993 followed by The Folkstone Collection in 1994, The Dollstone Collection and The Shoe Box Bears in 1996, and the DeskAnimals in 1998. Every new offering from Boyds has been received with enthusiasm and delight by a fiercely loyal and rapidly growing group of hundreds and thousands and millions of fans.

THE BEARSTONE COLLECTION

The first-born set of resin figurines was a collection of intricately detailed bears and hares that are a bit rough around the edges, giving them the rustic appeal of a well-loved teddy bear. These original pieces have multiplied to include a bevy of heartwarming characters in various life situations from gardening to graduation. These bears, cats, hares, dogs and occasional moose delight us with a spiffy fashion sense and a lust for life that only adds to the appeal of it all.

This season, it's raining Boyds as the *Noah's Pageant Series* sails into the collection. With four pieces making their debut this year, four new pieces will be issued each year until the final act in 2001.

Since its introduction in 1993, The Bearstone Collection has accumulated 322 pieces – 39 of them are new this season. In addition to the figurines, the collection also includes a variety of clocks, frames, music boxes, ornaments, plaques, votive holders, waterglobes and pins. Most of the pieces are produced in a particular quantity per edition – the magic number for each Bearstone edition is 3,600. However, the members of the *Holiday Pageant Series* and *Noah's Pageant Series* have 7,200 pieces in each edition.

THE FOLKSTONE COLLECTION

In the folk art style of pencil figurines, much of The Folkstone Collection is a tall, thin and "proud-of-it" assortment of personalities – from the angelic to the amphibious. The 34 new pieces for the spring season bring the total number of Folkstones to 265, with an edition size of 3,600 pieces each. In addition to a collection of traditional figurines, this eclectic branch of the family tree also includes several series.

The *Carvers Choice* series is a collection of resin folk art pieces with the look of hand-carved wood. The *Santa & Friends* series, consisting of five large Santas that were issued from 1994 through 1997, offers collectors a smaller way to complement a holiday display.

The Wee Folkstones series (9,600 pieces per edition) features faeries, angels in training, snowpeople and other "wee companions" that are designed to be perched on a shelf, on the ledge of a window or even on a soup can in the kitchen!!! Included with the angels in training are a group of Not Quite Guardian Angels (or "N.Q.G.A.") which add humorous touches with their clever but appropriate names. For example, "Birdie Holeinone . . . NQGA of Golfers" stands ready to direct your golf ball toward that pesky hole! A subgroup of *The Wee Folkstones* is *Ribbit & Co.*, a set of frogs in search of kisses, flies and a good bottle of wine.

In 1998, Boyds issued a gardening-themed trio of Liddy Pearl limited editions – a figurine, a frame and a waterglobe. While Lowenthal jokes that this was because he was running dry on creative new ideas, collectors found this grouping "TERRIFIC!!," and were left wondering and hoping that themed releases would become a more prominent characteristic of the line.

THE DOLLSTONE COLLECTION

The main characters in this collection are images of children with their dolls or teddy bears. In scenes of wide-eyed innocence and make-believe, these boys and girls remind us of a time when tea parties and magic shows were the best part of the day. This season, 19 new pieces were added to The Dollstone Collection of figurines, musicals, porcelain dolls, votive holders and waterglobes for a total of 81 pieces.

These smoothly finished pieces depicting "Yesterday's Child" were initially introduced to collectors in 1995 on QVC, the home shopping network, and were then made available in retail stores in 1996 in edition sizes of 4,800 pieces. QVC has been the showcase for premiering a variety of Dollstone pieces, called Premier Editions, ever since. Recently, introductions of Dollstone ornaments and San Francisco Music Boxes featuring the Dollstone children have delighted the nostalgic Boyds collector.

THE SHOE BOX BEARS

The Grizberg family of bears was introduced in 1996 with edition sizes of 6,000 each. This collection of Shoe Box Bears was appropriately named because Lowenthal, as a young boy, kept his small toys and treasures in shoe boxes. There are now a total of 15 Shoe Box animals (yes, there has even been a hare infiltration!) and it's easy to become a "Box" addict. Since these characters have limbs that are connected to their bodies with rubber bands, they are poseable. And while the original Shoe Box Bears sported spiffy collars and ties, the more recent additions adorn detailed outfits.

The Desk Animals

Most of us have a desk. It might be at your job in a high-powered office downtown or in the bedroom or den at home where you try to control the bill flow. To personalize these areas and create a mental escape of sorts, we often try to find cute and conversation-provoking items to display. Since 1998, Boyds has provided 10 such items, including a set exclusive to QVC, in the form of DeskAnimals.

These charming multi-piece animals are designed to appear as though they are submerged underwater, on their way to the other side of the river or caught mid-stream in the middle of a lazy float on the current. Appealing to the rustic, wild side in all of us, often with a sense of whimsy, the DeskAnimals include a variety of animals which include a well-racked moose, a legendary monster and a hippopotamus with a mouth large enough to insert your business cards (well, almost!).

Boyds Looks Ahead

With the "Head Bean Hisself" turning 50 this year, one can only imagine the surprises he is planning for himself and for his legions of fans and friends. Lowenthal's designing vision, which may appear a bit skewed and off-center, has allowed collectors to enjoy a slightly different view of life, though the expressive little eyes of the Boyds animals. Read on for a look at the collection which influenced the birth of the Boyds resin figurines – the Boyds plush animals!

Sneak Peek At Boyds Plush Animals

*E*very so often, a partnership forms between two great minds that changes history forever . . . Lewis and Clark were pioneers of exploration, Abbott and Costello took comedy to a whole new level and Orville and Wilbur Wright discovered the wonder of aviation. Gary Lowenthal and Gae Sharp served as visionaries in the field of collectibles, designing the jointed teddy bear who would become the basis for the characters of The Boyds Collection Ltd.

Since then, Boyds plush animals have expanded to include over 1,000 different plush designs, ranging from the traditional (bears, hares and cats) to the less conventional (elephants, pigs, gorillas and more). Here's a look at some of the more important features of the Boyds plush line:

Limited Editions

"Bailey," named for Lowenthal's daughter, and her friends "Emily " and "Edmund," have become three of the most popular pieces in the collection. The three have been released twice a year (in the Spring and in the Fall) every year since 1992 to model a new themed wardrobe for the season and charm collectors everywhere. In 1996, Bailey's brother "Matthew" joined the well-dressed clan, although he is only offered in the Fall season, because, as the "Head Bean" explains, "by the time he gets around to him, G.M. is just too pooped to design." And like any faithful pooch, the family dog "Indy" was not far behind, making his debut in 1997. Each piece is retired after one year's production to make room for an all-new collection of lovable limited editions.

Exclusives

In addition to their regular line of products, Boyds releases a wide range of exclusive pieces, which are only available through select outlets. These pieces are hard to

track down as they can be found in a wide variety of locations, ranging from major department stores such as Dillards and Lord & Taylor to small boutiques and catalogs. QVC, the television home shopping network, is also one of the largest and most popular dealers of Boyds exclusives. These pieces are quite the elusive little critters and often, collectors are not even aware that they exist. And by the time they do discover them, it's too late as production of exclusive pieces is limited to the season in which they are introduced.

ACCESSORIES

Do you know what your bears and hares do when you leave the house? To keep them out of mischief, Boyds has designed a plethora of accessories for your bears to play with while you're gone. Don't be surprised to come home and find your bears playing "dress up" in a multitude of sweaters and dresses or preparing a gourmet meal with their own bear-sized kitchen appliances. Never fear, with such a variety of accessories to choose from, your animals will never be bored again.

PLUSH SERIES

While every plush animal is different in its own way, Boyds has grouped animals with similar characteristics into categories to make them easier to identify. There are 23 categories in all, and each category has its own unique qualities. Some of the larger Boyds plush animal series include:

Animal Menagerie ... Just like the name implies, this is a collection of the more unique animals in the collection. Donkeys, elephants, gorillas, and pigs are just a sample of the animals you'll find in this barnyard.

Archive Series ... Designed in the style of the antique jointed teddy bear, several of these elegant animals are named after characters from merry old England.

SNEAK PEEK AT BOYDS PLUSH ANIMALS

Bears In The Attic... Perfect for hugging, these bears, hares and friends are made of soft stuffing to be extra floppy. While extremely durable, these pieces were created to have the look of well-loved toys from years ago.

Clintons Cabinet ... Named after the president's family and some of his advisors, many of these pieces have already retired.

J.B. Bean & Associates ... Fully poseable, these bears, hares, cats, dogs, etc. are filled with bean pellets and are fully jointed. Known as the "Board of Directors," these characters bring a bit of sophistication to the collection.

Mohair Bears ... Referred to by the Head Bean as "Upah Clahss, yet Affordable," these bears, hares, and most recently, cats are limited to six months or one year of production. These elite characters all come with suede paws, extra hard stuffing and handwritten tags and are packed in special boxes (a teddy condo of sorts). The bears are named for U.S. Presidents, while the hares are named for First Ladies.

Snow Bears ... Like their name implies, these bears of the arctic are all white, and often have irresistible, bright blue eyes. However, their whimsical expressions are sure to warm the chill in any heart.

T.F. Wuzzies ... The lovable *T.F. Wuzzies* got their name because of their lack of hair. These bears are made of heavy-duty fabric and are made to resemble the delicate mini bears that are on the market today – but at a less expensive price. While all under 5" tall, the *T.F. Wuzzies* are a giant hit among collectors.

T.J.'s Best Dressed ... The largest of the series, these super-models of the plush fashion scene each sport stylish outfits that mirror their distinctive personalities.

INSIDE THE WACKY WORLD OF BOYDS

Boyds

If you've ever seen a Bearstone figurine and especially if you've ever seen the "Head Bean Hisself," you know that The Boyds Collection Ltd. is not quite like any other collection.

AND NOW FOR THE GNUS...

There are several reasons for the unique, lighthearted, widespread appeal of the Boyds line. Not the least of which is Lowenthal's offbeat personality which has carried over into his product lines and folksy newsletter, "The Boyds Retail Inquirer," which is written by none other than the "Head Bean Hisself." This newspaper is an entertaining glimpse into the mind that designs these whimsical characters. Here, you'll find such headlines as: "News Flash! News Flash! . . . The Head Bean Survives Collectors' Expo With All Body Parts Intact!" Only after reading this publication can one begin to understand the artistic force behind a Folkstone creation named "Indulgenia Q. Bluit . . . Angel of Denial."

ROCK STAR GARY...

As a result of his immense popularity with the Boyds fans and followers, creator Gary Lowenthal has emerged with a kind of "rock star" image in the world of collectors. His appearances at collector shows require crowd control at which the hot ticket is the admittance to "Head Bean" signings and an always rousing and rowdy "Head Bean Chat," an informational, highly interactive question-and-answer seminar. Another increasingly popular venue for a Lowenthal "sighting" is on the home shopping television network QVC. This season celebrates his fifth year on the show as co-host with Senior Program Host Mary Beth Roe.

HOLY DECOYS, DUCKMAN ...

Before the birth of what is known today as The Boyds Collection Ltd., Gary Lowenthal began his foray into the wilderness of collectibles with hand-carved duck decoys. A perfectionist, Gary once told QVC viewers that he tried to give his decoys a "used" look by shooting them full of holes. Unfortunately, he only succeeded in blowing them apart.

BOYDS HISTORY 101 ...

However, Lowenthal soon got the hang of creating collectibles and the rest is history. Speaking of which, many of his resin, as well as plush pieces, take their names from historical characters. The Bearstone Collection rules with "Elizabeth . . . I Am The Queen" while "Stonewall . . . The Rebel" stands proudly, ready to defend equality between bears, hares and all others. A particular Folkstone, "Ernest Hemmingmoose . . . The Hunter" bears a resemblance to a literary hero, known for his passion for hunting.

A MATTER OF CHOICE ...

An observant collector may notice that certain pieces released in a particular season may look quite similar, but will have a different name (although matching phrase) and obvious design differences. These pieces come about due to a disagreement of sorts. During the production process if the "Head Bean" can't decide which design he likes best, he will turn to the Boyds employees for their opinion. After hearing their thoughts, he may find that he disagrees, so both pieces will be put on the production schedule, with his pick released as a limited edition known as "G.M.'s Choice."

Inside The Wacky World Of Boyds

Don't Quote Me On That ...

One of the most interesting and thought-provoking aspects of the Boyds resin figurines are the quotations, often historical themselves, which are found on the bottoms of the pieces. One can find a figurine that is appropriate for almost any occasion, and when you take a peek at the quote on the bottom, it usually emphasizes the overall message of the piece. Quotes can be found that are attributed to Abraham Lincoln, Mother Teresa and even great philosophers such as Confucius and even G. M. Lowenthal, himself (oops . . . Hisself!). Here are some memorable highlights:

"Love comforteth like sunshine after rain."
– Shakespeare on "Bailey ... Heart's Desire"

"Give me golf clubs, the fresh air and a beautiful partner and you can keep my golf clubs and the fresh air."
– Jack Benny on "Ziggy ... The Duffer"

"It does not matter how slowly you go as long as you do not stop."
– Confucius on "Pearl ... The Knitter"

"A person's got to believe in something. I believe I'll have another drink."
– W.C. Fields on "Amelia's Enterprise ... Carrot Juice"

"A moment on the lips ... A lifetime on the hips."
– Smith & Murray on "Ms. Griz ... Saturday Night"

"What is a Friend? A single soul dwelling in two bodies."
– Aristotle on "Victoria With Samantha ... Victorian Ladies"

"The acme of judicial distinction means the ability to look a lawyer straight in the eyes for two hours and not hear a damned word he says."
– Justice John Marshall on "Judge Griz ... Hissonah"

"If you can't say anything good about someone, sit right here by me."
– Alice Roosevelt Longworth on "Elizabeth ... I Am The Queen"

*G*ary Lowenthal is undoubtedly one of the most recognized and adored artists in the collectibles business. Boyds fans can't get enough of his zany "slightly off-centered" personality, or the whimsical bears, hares and other critters that he creates. There's quite a story behind the creative genius of The Boyds Collection Ltd. and only by flipping through the chapters of his life, can collectors gain insight into the world of "The Head Bean Hisself."

After growing up in Manhattan, Lowenthal graduated from Alfred University in upstate New York with a degree in biology and then headed for the Fiji Islands with the U.S. Peace Corps where he taught everything from science to sports. And then it was back to New York City where he spent seven years as a purchasing, design and merchandising representative for Bloomingdales.

But other dreams awaited Lowenthal, and in 1979, he and his wife Justina moved to Boyds, Maryland, where they opened an antiques store. And so began the Lowenthal foray into the world of collectibles with some hand-carved duck decoys and ceramic houses which he called "Gnomes Homes." The next step was the production of plush bears and the rest is history.

Since that first bear was created, the plush line has grown to over 1,000 different styles and has been joined by five resin collections. The Bearstone Collection debuted in 1993, The Folkstone Collection was added in 1994, while The Dollstone Collection and The Shoe Box Bears hit stores in 1996. In 1998, the DeskAnimals swam into the line.

Family Man Vs. Business Man

One of the most important facets of Gary Lowenthal's life is his family. There's his wife Justina, daughter Bailey, son Matthew and of course Indy, the family dog. If these names sound familiar to you, it's because Gary has designed several pieces as tributes to his family, giving collectors that special feeling of having been a part of the Lowenthal tribe as it has grown over the years.

Collectors really appreciate this focus on family values. As Jean Ann Sovereign of Missouri puts it, "He advises his collectors to 'buy responsibly' and to remember that your health and your family are the truly important things in your life. That's a message that you don't hear from corporate leaders very often, it's refreshing and it's honest and it's Gary."

> **"At signings, [Gary] speaks to you as much as time permits . . . Heck, he's more friendly than lots of my relatives!"**

In keeping with his strong sense of family, Lowenthal has maintained a "mom-and-pop store" mentality despite the phenomenal success of The Boyds Collection Ltd. This is yet another trait that collectors have not overlooked as Julie Christensen of Iowa observes: "It's rare that someone in his position remembers what it's like to be 'the little guy' and not lose sight of who got you where you are today."

So while Gary Lowenthal may not have gotten too big for his britches, it seems as though his britches may have gotten too big for him. In April 1998, the investment firm of Kohlberg, Kravis and Roberts (KKR) acquired The Boyds

Collection Ltd. Retailers and collectors alike wondered what would happen to the collection and the owner that they fell in love with when the "corporate world" stepped in. However, Lowenthal stepped up to assure everyone that all would be well and in fact, he just needed help in running such a large company. In fact, this agreement would actually allow the artist to step away from all the technicalities and politics of the business world and focus on what it was that he really enjoyed: cultivating his creative genius.

Collector Shari Martin of Ohio comments, "Sometimes he even points out the flaws in his products. That endears me to him even more." It is that commitment to perfection that has made Lowenthal's creations such a success. He has been known to retire a piece on the spot or change its color if its appearance does not live up to his expectations. Many Dollstones with less-than-perfect eyes have fallen victim to such a fate. The Head Bean knows the quality of work that his collectors have come to expect, and he is no way willing to let them down.

**ISN'T IT NIFTY?
THE HEAD BEAN
IS 50!**

On February 9, 1999 Gary Lowenthal celebrated half a century of nuttiness! Collectors who want to send Gary best wishes, (or sympathy cards) should send mail to:

That Nifty Fifty (Old) Guy
Who Runs The Joint
The Boyds Collection Ltd.
P.O. Box 4386
Gettysburg, PA 17325-4386

This commitment has truly paid off. In 1998, The Boyds Collection Ltd. won The Collectors' Choice Award for "Best Manufactured Teddy Bears" as well as several achievement awards from the National Association of Limited Edition Dealers (NALED). And The Head Bean Hisself earned the honor of becoming the "Central Pennsylvania Entrepreneur of the Year." This comes on the heels of his 1997 "Artist of the Year" NALED award. In addition, Boyds pieces have won several Golden Teddy and TOBY awards. Both "Corinna" and "Noah and Co . . . Ark Builders" were honored with the 1996 TOBY Public's Choice Award from *Teddy Bear And Friends* magazine, while "Neville . . . Compubear" followed suit in 1997.

EXCUSE ME SIR, CAN YOU SPARE A NAME?

During an episode of the QVC Boyds Bears Show, Lowenthal revealed that the quite unique names of some Boyds bears were originally chosen by walking up to people on the street and asking what their great grandmother's and great grandfather's names were.

A Ladies' Man, A Man's Man, A Collector's Man

One thing is for sure and that is that Lowenthal is well aware of the importance of collectors. His signings often take hours as he takes the time to talk with each and every collector. "He *listens* to what the collectors want," says Kristin Sheaffer of Georgia, "and takes their opinions to heart. He also shares a part of himself, and is not cold and distanced like some who have become successful."

With his friendly and easygoing attitude, it is no surprise that Boyds fans fly several hundred miles and wait hours in line to meet and have their pieces signed by "Yer Ol' Uncle Bean" at the few personal appearances he makes throughout the year. And these fans are never disappointed as Linda Reinhart of Pennsylvania remembers: "We were at the Hartville signing [Hartville Collectibles in Ohio, 10/10/98] . . . and Gary was the same zany, crazy, lovable Head Bean Hisself from the first Boyds lover's signed bears to the last four hours later." Perhaps Melissa Gabbard of Illinois says it best when she says, "He seems like a down to earth, regular guy. He doesn't act like a big-shot millionaire.

At signings, he speaks to you as much as time permits, takes photos with you, etc. In general, you feel like you're meeting a neighbor and friend. Heck, he's more friendly than lots of my relatives!"

"Because of him and his collection of wonderful, personable plush and stones, I have made friends all over the United States. These are not just people I have a casual relationship with, these are true friends!"

In addition to the personal appearances that he does every year, The Head Bean appears for a five-show miniseries (one episode per week) each year on QVC, the television home shopping network. The Boyds Bear Show, co-hosted by Senior Program Host Mary Beth Roe and Lowenthal, is one of  the most popular shows on QVC. Pieces sell out within minutes, if not seconds. So what makes these shows so popular? Annmarie Pearlstein of Arizona has an idea: "It is as much fun watching *him* [Gary], as well as seeing what kind of product he has to sell. He really enjoys his products, and projects that off on his customers."

Definitely not camera-shy, Lowenthal really lets his zaniness shine through on these television appearances, to the delight of his fans. Pearlstein recounts, "First off, you never know what he will be wearing! During the Christmas series, he came out dressed as an angel, a pilgrim and a Russian man." And she adds that during another show, "Gary came out very formally dressed and started to undress

while he was presenting his bears! By the end, he was just in a swimming trunk and sandals!" These appearances give the collector yet another glimpse (an often almost too revealing one) into the mind of the creator behind The Boyds Collection Ltd.

But while the show is very amusing for collectors, it's not all just fun and games. Pearlstein comments, "He also brings a very smart and savvy sales pitch through his humor, making his collectibles all the more irresistible." Therefore, not only is the show a great source of entertainment, it is great retail resource for collectors.

While people worldwide are thankful to Gary for the wonderful bears he creates, Linda Stratton of Texas, who has joined an on-line Boyds club has another reason to be thankful. "Because of him and his collection of wonderful, personable plush and stones, I have made friends all over the United States. These are not just people I have a casual relationship with, these are true friends! People I can count on, pour my heart out to, meet in various cities all over and know that they are just what they seem on my computer screen, my friend. That we collect Boyds is just a bonus, one more thing we have in common."

So what lies ahead for The Boyds Collection Ltd. and its offbeat head honcho? While it's impossible to predict the future, one thing is for sure and that is that as long as "Yer ol' Uncle Bean" is around, the Boyds family tree will continue to grow and to prosper.

THE BEARSTONE COLLECTION

This section highlights the new Boyds resin releases for Spring 1999.

FIGURINES

Alexandra & Belle ... "Telephone Tied" ... We have all felt "tied to the telephone" at one time or another and this duo is – literally! Even though this probably isn't exactly what Alexander Graham Bell had in mind, this talkative pair is all wrapped up in the invention.

Arnold P. Bomber ... The Duffer ... While he's not exactly on his way to winning the trophy, Arnold seems to have all the required paraphernalia for the game, including his trusty caddy. After his first swing, the ball is truly out-of-sight, but that's only because it's somewhere they're not looking – still resting comfortably on the tee. Those who missed their shot when this piece was an Early Release will feel victorious in finding it now in the general line.

Bailey ... The Bride ... For those who have watched Bailey grow up over the years, this will be a momentous figurine. While a wedding is supposed to be a once-in-a-lifetime event, collectors will be glad that this one was not if they missed this vision in white's debut as an Early Release.

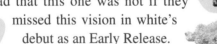

Bumble B. Bee ... Sweeter Than Honey ... This little guy actually thinks he can fool the bees with his clever disguise. Although his antennae make

him look a bit "out of this world," Bumble has actually succeeded in acquiring a mug of honey and some hungry
companions.

Caren B. Bearlove ... This adorable figurine is a great way
to show anyone that you "care" and "love" them.
However, as it is a GCC exclusive, Caren will only be able
to touch the hearts of those lucky enough to find her.

Chrissie ... Game, Set, Match ... Conserving her energy to take
on the next opponent, Chrissie cradles
the tools of her trade – a tennis
racket and ball. Although she
appears demure in her denim and
beige tennis togs, this little bear has
studied up on the rules of the game
and will prove to be quite a match!

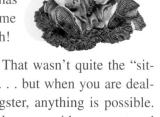

Flash McBear & The Sitting ... That wasn't quite the "sitting" that was expected . . . but when you are deal-
ing with a fidgety youngster, anything is possible.
Flash tries to distract and amuse with a puppet and
even a bottle, but "bottoms up" is all he got!

Gary, Tina, Matt & Bailey ... From Our Home To Yours ... In
celebration of their 20th year in the world of collectibles, this
figurine features Gary Lowenthal and his
family coming together to show
what has enabled the company to
grow and prosper – quality products combined with strong family
values. Displaying the chronology
of the line from the days of the duck
decoy to the bear, this piece will serve
as a great piece of Boyds history.

However, as it is limited to 1999 production, collectors will
have to act fast before it too becomes a piece of nostalgia.

WHAT'S NEW FOR BOYDS RESIN FIGURINES

Victoria Regina Buzzbruin ... So Many Flowers, So Little Time ...
This Special Event Piece features Victoria, The Queen Bee, and Junior Buzzbruin sitting beside a large sunflower and a homey beehive as Victoria cordially offers a plateful of yummy honeycombs.

Wanda & Gert ... A Little Off The Top ...
This could be a hairy situation if this bear beautician gets carried away. But with a tube of pomade, a can of "moose" and a "hare dryer" nearby, this little trim should come out looking just marvelous.

Noah's Pageant Series

Bernice As Mrs. Noah ... Chief Cook ... If behind every good man is a good woman and the best way to a man's heart is through his stomach, then this loyal wife is facing quite a challenge herself (not to mention the challenge of estimating the serving size for an elephant). Mrs. Noah looks well prepared for the task with her apron pockets bulging with tools and her cookbook in hand.

Jeremy As Noah ... The Ark Builder ... The master architect has all the necessary items at his feet to design his seaworthy, floating zoo. However, the little boat that he holds in his hand looks barely big enough to house his guests, so with a pencil behind his ear, it's back to the drawing board.

S. S. Noah ... The Ark ... Noah has finished his masterpiece and prepares to board and welcome the pairs of animals he is expecting. A sign on front helps to welcome all animals and one warns that there will be no

raincheck. Another promises that it will be quite a trip with events such as a "couples dance" and an inspirational one above the door reminds us all to "Believe."

Stretch & Skye ... The Lookouts ... These two gangly giraffes are literally supporting each other in their appointed roles as Noah's sentinels, keeping watch for the creatures coming two by two.

Other Pieces

Frames ... In "Bailey . . . Life Is A Daring Adventure," Boyds offers the advice that even in the roughest of waters, life should be an enterprise, while "Rocky . . . All Star" is sure to attain the same goal of delighting collectors as its figurine counterpart has.

Musicals ... In "Daphne And Eloise . . . Women's Work," these two hares study up on the essentials of a trip to the market, while in "Ms. Bruin & Bailey . . . The Lesson," a bit of caring (and a little snack) are incorporated into learning the A, B, C's.

Votive Holders ... "Noah . . . And The Golden Rule" carries the flame of inspiration as it reminds us all to "Do Unto Others . . . As You Would Have Them Do Unto You."

Waterglobes ... The two pals featured in "Elvira & Chauncey . . . Shipmates" demonstrate that their friendship will remain from "Timbuktu" to "The End Of The Earth."

Pins ... This season Boyds offers 17 new pins based on themes mirroring those of popular figurines, as well as the "Queen Bee" event pin that will send collectors buzzing to find her. In addition to these pieces, The Boyds Collection Ltd. has released a series of bloom pins that in comparison will make any real-life corsage look wilted.

✺ THE FOLKSTONE COLLECTION ✺

FIGURINES

Audubon P. Pussywillow ... The Birdwatcher ... After having studied the "Boyds Guide to The Birds," or at least standing proudly beside it, this feline ornithologist has birdseed and binoculars in paw and is ready to go shoot some birds. But they have nothing to fear, as his relaxed companion attests, the only shooting to be done will be with a camera.

Domestica T. Whirlwind ... NQGA Of Super Moms ... Domestica has this "mom" thing down pat. She can cook, clean, answer the phone and complete her "To Do" list in the nick of time (notice her multiple wrist watches). Domestica is the perfect inspirational companion for anyone who knows that being a mom is a full-time job.

Harriet & Punch With Hermaine ... The Challenge ... "No strain, no gain . . ." is easy for these hares to say, but it's the chicken that needs to be up to the challenge. This chicken seems to be holding up just fine as she sits high atop the results of her monumental task.

Laverne B. Bowler ... Strikes & Spares ... Reflecting upon the innocence of the days of poodle skirts and monogrammed sweaters, Laverne faces what might be the biggest challenge of

the times – the "7-10" split. Yet as she prepares to head for the lane, she stands on a message of pure confidence.

Ms. Fries ... Guardian Angel Of Waitresses ... So that's how waitresses succeed in delivering your order in a flash – they have rollerskates and two sets of wings! Those collectors who were left hungry when this piece sold out as an Early Release will satisfy their appetites when their order is filled through the regular line.

Ms. McFrazzle ... Daycare Extraordinaire ... As anyone who has ever cared for a child knows, Ms. McFrazzle deserves that halo for her efforts. Having to be a master of everything from child psychology to removing a lollipop from a sweater, this harried bear waits anxiously for that watch to read 5 o'clock.

Myron R. Fishmeister ... Angel of Fish Stories ... Myron has found a way to combine creative storytelling with the sport of fishing. His willing assistant is ready to substantiate any fish tale that he may come up with – after all, you need witnesses for that "one that got away!"

Wendy Willowhare ... A Tisket A Tasket ... The old nursery rhyme that goes: "A tisket, a tasket, A red and yellow basket . . ." is brought to life in this charming figurine of Wendy with her collection of woven baskets – ready to fill with . . . ?

CARVERS CHOICE

Chester Bigheart ... Love Much ... Chester, the papa bear who is being smothered with kisses and love from his adoring cubs, personifies the quotation from George Sand that is found on the bottom of the piece: "There is only one happiness in life, to love and be loved." And while his love is unlimited, the figurine is not, as it is limited to 12,000 pieces.

Jester Q. Funnybones ... Laugh Often ... Jester has his little buddies in stitches, falling down with laughter. However, one has to wonder if the jokes might be even funnier if he weren't reading them upside down.

Lady Harriet Rushmore . . . Never Enough Time . . . A woman's work is never done and most women can relate to this image of Harriet rushing to her next appointment, clock in her hand and wind in her fur.

Sir Simon Steadfast ... Always Enough Time ... Simon, on the other hand, seems to have mastered the art of time management and always seems to find the time to stop and share a few minutes with anyone who requests it. Maybe he can take a moment to help out Lady Harriet.

Walter T. Goodlife ... Live Well ... Walter, all dressed up from his patriotic top hat and tails to the spats on his shoes, proudly exemplifies the good life. With his bag of coins, grin on his face and his companion making a toast, Walter looks ready to "share the wealth."

THE WEE FOLKSTONES

Confidentia "No-Tell" Faeriewhisper ... Shhh . . . don't worry, Confidentia will never divulge a secret told to her. In fact, she keeps them in a locked box and only you have the key!

Felicity Angelbliss... The Bride's Angel... A true vision in white, this piece sits high above the clouds in testimony to the lifting power of love. Interlocking rings inscribed with "Be Mine" sit nearby.

Fergus "Bogey" MacDivot... With tee in hand and ball on head, Fergus is ready to hit the green. However, it looks like he may be hitting it a bit too hard as he seems to have quite a divot forming around his feet.

Grandma Faeriehugs... This image of Grandma in her apron and slippers will warm your heart and make you smile. This piece will surely make anyone who sees it want to embrace it into their collection.

Tuxworth P. Cummerbund... Assigned to keep watch over the ring, Tuxworth will ensure that all goes as planned. But it's hard not to notice that mischievous glimpse in his eye – after all, weddings should be fun!

RIBBIT & CO.

Jeremiah "Jellybean" Pondhopper... While looking a bit greener than usual (perhaps he ate too many jellybeans), this would-be Easter Bunny cheerfully dons a costume to help welcome spring with pots of daffodils, tulips and hyacinth.

Ms. Lilypond... Lesson #1... "Look before you leap" is something we all should keep in mind, especially if you live on the "edge."

TuTu C. Ribbit...Frog Lake... In this rather swampy version of "Swan Lake," this ballerina "wanna-be" is really stretching it to the extreme by attempting to bring a little class to her waters!

OTHER PIECES

Frames... Try as he might, Frogmorton is unable to convince his little pal that a good catch is better than a good book in the *Ribbit & Co.* "Frogmorton & Tad . . . Fly Fishing." In the *Carvers Choice* frame "Martha Bigheart . . .

Love Much," Martha's arms envelope the images of all who are lucky enough to be "framed" by her heart.

Musicals... Die-hard chocolate lovers know that an extra large scoop is the only option when it comes to chocolate. In *The Wee Folkstones* musical "Cocoa M. Angelrich & Scoop," Cocoa is doing the scooping herself and is more than willing to give a little extra!

 Votive Holders . . . In "Audubon P. Pussywillow . . . The Birdwatcher," this sly feline burns with the desire to capture some birds, with a camera that is.

Pins... Based on familiar characters from all walks of Folkstone life, these pins are a must-have for any collection. With themes encompassing life lessons to well wishes, there is a pin to suit just about everyone.

❋ THE DOLLSTONE COLLECTION ❋

FIGURINES

Alyssa With Caroline ... A Stitch In Time ... Cross-stitching with a friend always makes work more enjoyable – and these two are also in sync with their message. Alyssa has stitched "Be" while Caroline has formed the word "Mine."

Heather With Lauren ... Bunny Helpers ... Easter is a busy time for a particular bunny, but luckily he has these two cuties who are decked out in their bunny suits (and bunny slippers!) ready to lend a hand (or paw).

Kelly And Company ... The Bear Collector ... A devoted bear collector, Kelly has found herself in the best of company: her stuffed friends! Surrounded by a plethora of sweet faces, as well as a book or two on collecting, she seems to be "keeping company" with all the right folks!

Lucinda And Dawn ... By The Sea ... These two friends remind us to pay attention to the simpler pleasures of life such as treasures found while beachcombing and the sweet sea serenade of the conch shell.

Melissa With Katie ...The Ballet ... In preparation for tonight's performance, these ballerinas make sure they're limber enough for their debut. It is not a far stretch to imagine the beautiful performance that they will put on.

Meredith With Jacqueline ... Daisy Chain ... The joy and beauty of picking daisies on a hot summer day is only equaled to that of friends making long chains out of the flowers for necklaces and crowns.

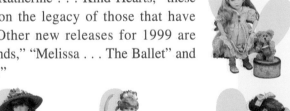

Stephanie With Jim ... School Days ... Stephanie shows her zest for learning, sitting with her hand raised in anticipation of being called on by her teacher. She has passed on her love of school to her buddy bear, Jim, who follows along in his book.

OTHER PIECES

Frames ... "Lindsey With Louise . . .The Recital" will be music to every collector's ears as it sings that the true measure of life is contentment.

Musicals... "Grace & Faith . . . I Have A Dream" offers the hope that we can all live in perfect harmony, no matter the color of our skin.

Porcelain Dolls... From a glass of freshly squeezed lemonade in "Erin . . . Lemonade For Two" to a dose of TLC in "Katherine . . . Kind Hearts," these beautiful dolls carry on the legacy of those that have come before them. Other new releases for 1999 are "Julia . . . Garden Friends," "Melissa . . . The Ballet" and "Wendy . . . Wash Day."

Votive Holders ... "Lucinda And Dawn . . . By The Sea" A battered and beach-worn bucket reminds collectors of the never ending beauty of the sea.

Waterglobes ... It will be love at first sight when collectors see the only available waterglobe in The Dollstone Collection, "Ryan & Diane . . . Love Is Forever."

 ## THE SHOE BOX BEARS

Ellie Grizberg ... Egg Hunter ... All dressed up in her bunny suit with a perky blue bow, Ellie is on the lookout for the colorful eggs that Momma has just decorated for the annual Easter egg hunt.

Momma Grizberg ... Egg Decorator ... With her paintbrushes in the pocket of her bunny suit, Momma is ready for the yearly task of egg beautification.

Sgt. Bookum O'Reilly ... To Protect & Serve ... This friendly neighborhood beat cop is ready for action with his ticket book in hand, ready for the next perpetrator.

DESKANIMALS

Puff Lochlegend...What is all that talk about the scary, mysterious creatures of the sea? This Loch Ness critter is nothing to be scared of and will make sea monster sightings much more enjoyable.

Puff & Nessie Lochlegend... It can get pretty lonely being an aquatic villain, but this floating fiend has found the monster of his dreams. The romantic duo in this exclusive QVC set will create their own legend as they swim into the sea of love, as well as into the homes of collectors.

Shelby Turtlecrawlius... In a water race, surely this guy would beat any hare, and by much more than a hair. However, judging from the look on his face, he's not too sure of his water prowess.

Spitz And Floyd Frogswimium ... Easy Method Swim School... Here's a new interpretation of the term "doggy paddle." Of course this is the "Easy Method Swim School," because for frogs, swimming is easy – as this helpful instructor assures his new student. However, much like his fellow water-dweller Bridges from *Ribbit & Co.*, the "beginner swimmer" doesn't seem to realize that because of his nature, a snorkel really isn't necessary. On the other hand, it does make him look pretty professional.

COLLECTOR'S CLUB NEWS

Collector's

Club

*I*n 1996, due to popular demand, a seed was planted and the Loyal Order of Friends of Boyds – a club exclusively for Boyds fans – began to grow. Now, in 1999, it blooms with a tale of Flora Mae Berriweather:

"Once upon a time in the Land of Boyds . . . lived Flora Mae Berriweather and her daughter Blossum. Flora was famous for her Green Thumb . . . she seemed to win all of the Blue Ribbons in Gardening at the Country Fair. Blossum wanted to plant a garden and be just like her Mom!"

The story continues with mother Flora imparting her gardening wisdom upon daughter Blossum, using these three inspirational phrases:

"Plant With Hope . . . Grow With Love . . . Bloom With Joy"

And this wisdom blossomed into the 1999 F.o.B. collector's club kit. For a yearly membership fee of $32.50 (yes, while the idea grew, the price did not!), collectors receive the following gifts:

***Blossum B. Berriweather . . . Bloom With Joy!* . . .** This exclusive Bearstone figurine shows young Blossum wearing her hat decorated with lovely sunflowers. She is standing under her pride and joy – a gigantic sunflower (measuring over 4" tall!)

***Flora Mae Berriweather* . . .** This 6" plush bear is dressed in a pale yellow hand-knit cardigan sweater, a brown neck bow and a yellow felt hat whose large silk sunflower makes the perfect finishing touch to the outfit.

***"Bloomin' F.o.B." 1999 Bearstone Pin* . . .** This isn't just any old piece of jewelry, it's a symbol to everyone that the wearer is a proud F.o.B.!

***One Year's Subscription to the "F.o.B. Inquirer"* . . .** This newspaper is penned by the "Head Bean Hisself." This allows members to be the first to know what's happening in the world of Boyds. And starting this year, this publication will be issued four times (an increase of two issues per year)!

Genuine F.o.B. Sunflower Seed Packet... Hopefully, members have been listening carefully to their gardening lesson as this club perk gives them a chance to put it to good use and create some of their own outdoor beauty.

The knowledge of what to look for and where to look for it with...

• Boyds Bears & Friends Product List and
  Color Catalog Order Form

• Boyds Bears & Friends Dealer Directory

The opportunity to purchase these exclusive Members Only pieces...

• "Sunny And Sally Berriweather . . .
  Plant With Hope" *(Bearstone Figurine)*

• "Plant With Hope, Grow With Love,
  Bloom With Joy" *(Plush Bears)*

• "Noah's Genius At Work Table" *(Noah's Pageant Series)*

• 1999 Official F.o.B. Mug

To join the club, all you have to do is check with your retailer or fill out the application in the back of the Collector's Value Guide, submit payment ($32.50), drop it in an envelope and mail to:

In addition to the officially sponsored club, local clubs for Boyds fans are popping up all over the place. Check with your retailer to find out if there is one in your hometown. Or even how to start your own!

THE LOYAL ORDER OF FRIENDS OF BOYDS
The Boyds Collection Ltd.
P. O. Box 4386, F.o.B. Dept.
Gettysburg, PA 17325-4386

FUTURE RETIREMENTS

Retirements

$\mathscr{T}$he following is a list of the Bearstones, Folkstones and Dollstones that are scheduled to be retired by December 31, 1999. Don't start the millennium without them because they may be impossible to find after January 1, 2000! Their issue years and item numbers are in parentheses.

RETIRING IN 1999!

THE BEARSTONE COLLECTION

Figurines

- ❏ Angelica . . . The Guardian (1995, #2266)
- ❏ Caren B. Bearlove (1999, #227722GCC)
- ❏ Daphne & Eloise . . . Women's Work (1995, #2251)
- ❏ Emma & Bailey . . . Afternoon Tea (1996, #2277)
- ❏ Gary, Tina, Matt & Bailey . . . From Our Home To Yours (1999, #227804)
- ❏ Grenville & Beatrice . . . Best Friends (1994, #2016)
- ❏ Homer On The Plate (1994, #2225)
- ❏ Justina & M. Harrison . . . Sweetie Pies (1994, #2015)
- ❏ Kringle & Bailey With List (1994, #2235)
- ❏ M. Harrison's Birthday (1996, #2275)
- ❏ Ms. Griz . . . Monday Morning (1996, #2276)
- ❏ Sir Edmund . . . Persistence (1996, #2279)
- ❏ Victoria Regina Buzzbruin . . . So Many Flowers, So Little Time (1999, #01999-71)
- ❏ Victoria . . . The Lady (1993, #2004)

Holiday Pageant Series

- ❏ Ariel & Clarence . . . As The Pair O' Angels (1997, #2411)
- ❏ Baldwin . . . As The Child (1995, #2403)
- ❏ Bruce . . . As The Shepherd (1997, #2410)
- ❏ Caledonia . . . As The Narrator (1998, #2412)
- ❏ Essex . . . As The Donkey (1997, #2408)
- ❏ Heath . . . As Caspar (1996, #2405)
- ❏ Matthew . . . As The Drummer (1998, #2415)
- ❏ Ms. Bruin . . . As The Teacher (1998, #2414)
- ❏ Neville . . . As Joseph (1995, #2401)
- ❏ Raleigh . . . As Balthasar (1996, #2406)
- ❏ Serendipity . . . As The Guardian Angel (1998, #2416)
- ❏ The Stage . . . School Pageant (1995, #2425)
- ❏ Thatcher & Eden . . . As The Camel (1996, #2407)
- ❏ Theresa . . . As Mary (1995, #2402)
- ❏ Wilson . . . As Melchior (1996, #2404)
- ❏ Winkie & Dink . . . As The Lambs (1997, #2409)

Clocks
❏ Bailey . . . On Time
(1997, #27600)

Waterglobes
❏ Homer On The Plate
(1997, #270550)

Votive Holders
❏ Daphne . . . In The Cabbage Patch
(1997, #27750)
❏ Sebastian & Nicholas . . .
The Lost Ball (1998, #27753)

Bearwear Pins
❏ Grace . . . Born To Shop
(1997, #26010)
❏ Ms. Bruin . . . Learn!
(1998, #26111)
❏ Queen Bee (1999, #N/A)
❏ Wilson . . . Hugs & Kisses
(1997, #26011)

THE FOLKSTONE COLLECTION

Figurines
❏ Beatrice . . . The Giftgiver
(1995, #2836)
❏ Egon . . . The Skier (1996, #2837)
❏ Ernest Hemmingmoose . . .
The Hunter (1995, #2835)
❏ Flora, Amelia & Eloise . . .
The Tea Party (1996, #2843)
❏ Illumina . . . Angel of Light
(1996, #28203)
❏ Loretta Moostein . . . "Yer
Cheatin' Heart" (1996, #2854)
❏ Ziggy . . . The Duffer
(1997, #2838)

Carvers Choice
❏ Chester Bigheart . . . Love Much
(1999, #370053)

The Wee Folkstones
❏ Angelina "Smidge" Angellove . . .
Angel of True Love
(1997, #36100)
❏ Dentinata Faeriefloss . . . The
Tooth Faerie (1997, #36102)
❏ Gabrielle "Gabby" Faeriejabber
(1997, #36003)

Ribbit & Co.
❏ Bridges . . . Scuba Frog
(1998, #36751)

THE DOLLSTONE COLLECTION

Figurines

☐ Ashley With Chrissie . . .
Dress Up (1996, #3506)

Ma - ✗ ☐ Caitlin With Emma & Edmund . . .
Diapering Baby (1997, #3525)

☐ Candice With Matthew . . .
Gathering Apples (1996, #3514)

☐ Kelly And Company . . . The
Bear Collector (1999, #3542)

☐ Natalie With Joy . . . Sunday
School (1997, #3519)

☐ Patricia With Molly . . . Attic
Treasures (1996, #3501)

☐ Rachael, Barbara & Matthew . . .
Sabbath Lights (1998, #3526)

☐ Victoria With Samantha . . .
Victorian Ladies (1996, #3502)

Porcelain Dolls

☐ Erin . . . Lemonade For Two
(1999, #4915)

☐ Julia . . . Garden Friends
(1999, #4912)

☐ Katherine . . . Kind Hearts
(1999, #4910)

☐ Melissa . . . The Ballet
(1999, #4914)

☐ Wendy . . . Wash Day
(1999, #4909)

Votive Holders

☐ Whitney With Wilson . . .
Tea And Candlelight
(1997, #27950)

This section lists the ten most valuable pieces in The Bearstone Collection, as determined by their 1999 secondary market values. To qualify for this exclusive list, each piece must have top dollar value and show a significant percentage increase in value from its original retail price (as shown by our market meter). *Important note: All secondary market values listed in this section are for "1E" versions of the figurine.*

Christmas Bear Elf With List (#BC2051)

Issued 1994 – Retired 1994
Original Price: $24.99 (Can.)
Secondary Market Value: **1E** – $950 (U.S.)
Market Meter: +3,702%

This Canadian Exclusive was available in a limited edition of only 1,872 pieces. And as it was only available in Canada, it has become coveted by collectors everywhere. Because of the extreme rarity of this piece, "Christmas Bear Elf With List" is the most valuable figurine on the Boyds secondary market.

Grenville ... With Green Scarf (#2003-04)

Issued 1993 – Retired 1993
Original Price: $11
Secondary Market Value: **1E** – $620
Market Meter: +5,537%

This adorable figurine, one of the first to feature the popular Grenville, was also one of the first pieces in The Bearstone Collection. Unlike its companion piece "Grenville . . . With Red Scarf," the green-scarfed Grenville was only available for only one year.

Wilson With Love Sonnets (#2007)
Issued 1993 – Retired 1997
Original Price: $13
Secondary Market Value: **1E** – *$575*
Market Meter: +4,323%

This romantic bruin has resided in the Bearstone Top Ten for several years, even before his 1997 retirement. One of the first pieces introduced in the collection, this piece features Wilson with a giant book of love poems.

Grenville The Santabear (#2030)
Issued 1994 – Retired 1996
Original Price: $14.50
Secondary Market Value: **1E** – *$540*
Market Meter: +3,625%

This holiday piece featuring Grenville in his oversized hat and Santa costume captured collectors' hearts, making it a very hard piece to come by as a 1E.

Bailey Bear With Suitcase (#2000, rough version)
Issued 1993 – Current
Original Price: $14.50
Secondary Market Value: **1E** – *$525*
Market Meter: +3,521%

One of the few current pieces to make the most valuable list, this piece became a little rough over its lifespan. The "smooth" version had 11,000 pieces produced with the 1E mark, while the "rough" version had only 3,600 pieces with the 1E mark, making it the more valuable find.

Father Chrisbear And Son (#2008)
Issued 1993 – Retired 1993
Original Price: $14.50
Secondary Market Value: **1E** – *$495*
Market Meter: +3,314%

Only available for one year and with a very limited production quantity, this figurine was the first piece to depict a Christmas scene.

Clara ... The Nurse (#2231, original version)

Issued 1994 – Retired 1998
Original Price: $16
Secondary Market Value: **1E** – **$435**
Market Meter: +2,619%

While 1998 brought about the retirement of the resculpted version of this piece, it's the original version's first editions that fetch the highest secondary market value.

Grenville & Beatrice ... Best Friends (#2016)

Issued 1994 – To Be Retired 1999
Original Price: $26
Secondary Market Value: **1E** – **$425**
Market Meter: +1,535%

This piece, which is set to retire in 1999, was produced in two versions. The first edition ("1E") pieces show a dove on the right front side of the base, while later editions have the dove on the front center of the base.

Simone de Bearvoire & Her Mom, My Auntie Alice (#2001)

Issued 1993 – Retired 1996
Original Price: $14.50
Secondary Market Value: **1E** – **$365**
Market Meter: +2,418%

Several of these mother/daughter figurines were created without patches on the paws, a variation which commands a higher value than its patched counterpart.

Celeste ... The Angel Rabbit (#2230)

Issued 1994 – Retired 1997
Original Price: $16.50
Secondary Market Value: **1E** – **$350**
Market Meter: +2,022%

This heavenly figurine, one of the first hares produced in The Bearstone Collection, enjoys the honor of being the only non-bear in the Top Ten.

This section showcases the five most valuable pieces in The Folkstone Collection as determined by their values on the secondary market. In order to qualify for this section, the pieces must have top dollar value and show a significant increase in value from its original price (as shown by our market meter). *Important note: All secondary market values listed in this section are for "1E" versions of the figurine, unless it was produced without editions ("NE").*

Na-Nick And Siegfried ... The Plan (#2807)
Issued 1996 – Retired 1996
Original Price: $34
Secondary Market Value: NE – $160
Market Meter: +371%

December 26th (*Santa & Friends*, #3003)
Issued 1996 – Retired 1997
Original Price: $33
Secondary Market Value: 1E – $130
Market Meter: +294%

Nick On Ice (*Santa & Friends*, #3001, original version)
Issued 1994 – Retired 1997
Original Price: $33
Secondary Market Value: 1E – $117
Market Meter: +255%

Santa's Flight Plan (*Santa & Friends*, #3000, original version)
Issued 1994 – Retired 1997
Original Price: $33
Secondary Market Value: 1E – $116
Market Meter: +252%

Jingle Moose (#2830, original version)
Issued 1994 – Retired 1996
Original Price: $16
Secondary Market Value: 1E – $110
Market Meter: +588%

*T*his section features the five most valuable pieces in The Dollstone Collection, as determined by their secondary market values. These pieces are chosen by their dollar values and will show a percentage increase in value from its original price, as determined by our market meter. *Important note: All secondary market values listed in this section are for Premier Editon versions of the figurine.*

Jennifer With Priscilla ... The Doll In The Attic (#3500)
Issued 1996 – Retired 1997
Original Price: $20.50
Secondary Market Value: **PR** – $210
Market Meter: +925%

Patricia With Molly ... Attic Treasures (#3501)
Issued 1996 – To Be Retired 1999
Original Price: $14
Secondary Market Value: **PR** – $205
Market Meter: +1,365%

Katherine With Edmund & Amanda ... Kind Hearts (#3505)
Issued 1996 – Current
Original Price: $20
Secondary Market Value: **PR** – $168
Market Meter: +740%

Sarah & Heather With Elliot, Dolly & Amelia ... Tea For Four (#3507)
Issued 1996 – Retired 1996
Original Price: $47
Secondary Market Value: **PR** – $162
Market Meter: +245%

Mallory With Patsy & J.B. Bean ... Trick Or Treat (#3517)
Issued 1996 – Current
Original Price: $27
Secondary Market Value: **PR** – $160
Market Meter: +493%

1. LOCATE your piece in the Value Guide, which begins with Bearstones, followed by Folkstones, Dollstones, Shoe Box Bears, DeskAnimals and Collector's Club pieces. Within each section, figurines are found first, followed by an alphabetical listing of miscellaneous items such as music boxes and ornaments. To quickly locate a particular piece, use the *Bearfinder* indexes beginning on page 196.

	Values
1E	$98
2E	$72
3E	$58
AE	$28

Agatha & Shelly ... "Scaredy Cat"
#2246 • Original Price: $14.50
Issued: 1994 • Retired: 1998

2. LOOK on the bottom of your piece to determine its edition number. For more information on edition numbers, see the *Secondary Market Overview* on page 181.

3. FIND the market value of your piece. Note: You will find values listed for 1E's, 2E's and 3E's. "AE" refers to "all editions" 4E and higher, while "PR" refers to Premier Edition pieces. For current pieces, the "AE" value will be listed as the approximate current retail price. Items that do not have edition numbers (for example, some ornaments) will have only one market value listed as "NE." If a value is listed as "N/A," no such edition number exists for that piece and if its value is listed as "N/E," a secondary market value has yet to be established. For more information on pieces with variations, refer to the *Variations* feature on page 186.

4. RECORD both the original price that you paid and the current value of the piece, according to the edition number, in the corresponding boxes at the bottom of each page. Calculate the total value for the entire page by adding together all of the boxes in each column. Use a pencil so you can change the totals as your collection grows!

GENERAL FIGURINES		
Date Purchased	Price Paid	Value Of My Collection
1. *3/95*	*14.50*	*72*
2.		
3.		
4.		
PENCIL TOTALS		

5. TRANSFER the totals from each page to the "Total Value Of My Collection" worksheets beginning on page 178.

6. ADD all of the totals together to determine the overall value of your collection.

GENERAL FIGURINES

With 10 new additions to The Bearstone Collection this season, including a piece commemorating The Boyds Collection Ltd.'s 20th anniversary, this branch of the family tree has sprouted to a total of 130 pieces. Here you can find bears, hares, moose and many other familiar characters (even the "Head Bean Hisself") in a variety of situations including chatting on the phone and learning to fly.

①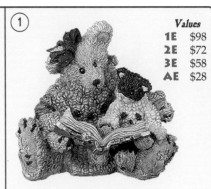

Values	
1E	$98
2E	$72
3E	$58
AE	$28

Agatha & Shelly ... "Scaredy Cat"
#2246 • Original Price: $14.50
Issued: 1994 • Retired: 1998

② New!

Values	
1E	$19
2E	$19
3E	$19
AE	$19

Alexandra & Belle ... "Telephone Tied"
#227720 • Original Price: $19
Issued: 1999 • Current

③

Value	
NE	$43

Alexis Bearinsky ... Twas The Night Before Christmas (GCC Early Release)
#228314GCC • Original Price: $24.50
Issued: 1998 • Retired: 1998

④

Values	
1E	$86
2E	$65
3E	$52
AE	$29

Amelia's Enterprise ... Carrot Juice
#2258 • Original Price: $16.50
Issued: 1995 • Retired: 1998

GENERAL FIGURINES

	Date Purchased	Price Paid	Value Of My Collection
1.			
2.			
3.			
4.			
PENCIL TOTALS			

1

Values	
1E	$74
2E	$53
3E	$42
AE	$26

Angelica ... The Guardian
#2266 • Original Price: $18.50
Issued: 1995 • Retired: 1998

2

New!

Values	
1E	$21
2E	$21
3E	$21
AE	$21
Variation	
NE	$36

Arnold P. Bomber ... The Duffer
#227714 • Original Price: $21
Issued: 1999 • Current
Variation: 1998 GCC Early Release

3

Values	
1E	$185
2E	$152
3E	$120
AE	$95

Arthur ... With Red Scarf
#2003-03 • Original Price: $11
Issued: 1993 • Retired: 1994

4

Values	
1E	$30
2E	$18.50
3E	$18.50
AE	$18.50
Variation	
1E	$77
2E	$54
3E	$43
AE	$18.50

Bailey & Becky ... The Diary (RS)
#228304 • Original Price: $18.50
Issued: 1997 • Current
Variation: original version

General Figurines

	Date Purchased	Price Paid	Value Of My Collection
1.			
2.			
3.			
4.			
PENCIL TOTALS			

BEARSTONES

① Values
1E	$164
2E	$108
3E	$92
AE	$73

Bailey & Emily...Forever Friends
#2018 • Original Price: $34
Issued: 1994 • Retired: 1996

② Values
1E	$295
2E	$165
3E	$124
AE	$45

Bailey & Wixie...
To Have And To Hold
#2017 • Original Price: $16
Issued: 1994 • Retired: 1998

③ Values
1E	$168
2E	$142
3E	$115
AE	$85

Bailey At The Beach
#2020-09 • Original Price: $16
Issued: 1994 • Retired: 1995

④ Values
1E	$525
2E	$355
3E	$270
AE	$14.50
Variation	
1E	$156
2E	N/A
3E	N/A
AE	N/A

Bailey Bear With Suitcase
#2000 • Original Price: $14.50
Issued: 1993 • Current
Variation: smooth fur, brown bottom

⑤ Values
1E	$100
2E	$65
3E	$50
AE	$15

Bailey...Heart's Desire
#2272 • Original Price: $15
Issued: 1996 • Current

GENERAL FIGURINES

	Date Purchased	Price Paid	Value Of My Collection
1.			
2.			
3.			
4.			
5.			
PENCIL TOTALS			

①

Values	
1E	N/A
2E	N/A
3E	N/A
AE	$63
Variation	
1E	$300
2E	$192
3E	$155
AE	$76

Bailey ... In The Orchard
#2006 • Original Price: $14.50
Issued: 1993 • Retired: 1996
Variation: paw print on jug

②

Values	
1E	$92
2E	$78
3E	$62
AE	$44

Bailey ... Poor Ol' Bear
#227704 • Original Price: $15
Issued: 1997 • Retired: 1997

③

Values	
1E	$24
2E	$13
3E	$13
AE	$13
Variation 1	
1E	$95
2E	$66
3E	$54
AE	$13
Variation 2	
1E	$310

Bailey The Baker ... With Sweetie Pie (RS)
#2254 • Original Price: $13
Issued: 1995 • Current
Variation 1: original version;
Variation 2: "Clarion Bear"

④ **New!**

Values	
1E	$18
2E	$18
3E	$18
AE	$18
Variation	
NE	$42

Bailey ... The Bride
#227712 • Original Price: $18
Issued: 1999 • Current
Variation: 1998 GCC Early Release
"Bailey ... As The Bride"

GENERAL FIGURINES

	Date Purchased	Price Paid	Value Of My Collection
1.			
2.			
3.			
4.			
✏ PENCIL TOTALS			

BEARSTONES

①

Values	
1E	$68
2E	$52
3E	$42
AE	$16

Bailey ... The Cheerleader
#2268 • Original Price: $16
Issued: 1995 • Current

②

Values	
1E	$29
2E	$17
3E	$17
AE	$17
Variation	
1E	$54
2E	$37
3E	$28
AE	$17

Bailey ... The Graduate – Carpe Diem (RS)
#227701-10 • Original Price: $17
Issued: 1997 • Current
Variation: original version

③

Values	
1E	$87
2E	$67
3E	$52
AE	$16

Bailey ... The Honey Bear
#2260 • Original Price: $16
Issued: 1995 • Current

④

Values	
1E	$220
2E	$133
3E	$100
AE	$16

Bailey's Birthday
#2014 • Original Price: $16
Issued: 1994 • Current

⑤

Values	
JAN	$100
FEB	$78
MAR	$63
APR-DEC	$57

Beatrice...We Are Always The Same Age Inside (LE-1998)
#227802 • Original Price: $48
Issued: 1998 • Retired: 1998

GENERAL FIGURINES

	Date Purchased	Price Paid	Value Of My Collection
1.			
2.			
3.	31E/9&3 Gift 99	Gift	
4.			
5.			
✏ PENCIL TOTALS			

①

Value
NE $35

Bee My Honey
(Parade Of Gifts Exclusive)
#94575POG • Original Price: $12
Issued: 1998 • Retired: 1998

②

	Values
1E	$98
2E	$72
3E	$60
AE	$48

Bessie The Santa Cow
#2239 • Original Price: $16
Issued: 1994 • Retired: 1996

③ New!

	Values
1E	$16
2E	$16
3E	$16
AE	$16

Bumble B. Bee...
Sweeter Than Honey
#227718 • Original Price: $16
Issued: 1999 • Current

④

	Values
1E	$54
2E	$39
3E	$32
AE	$18

Buzz... The Flash
#227706 • Original Price: $18
Issued: 1997 • Current

GENERAL FIGURINES

	Date Purchased	Price Paid	Value Of My Collection
1.			
2.			
3.			
4.			
5.			
✏ PENCIL TOTALS			

⑤

	Values
1E	N/A
2E	N/A
3E	N/A
AE	$92
	Variation
1E	$150
2E	$112
3E	$105
AE	N/A

Byron & Chedda With Catmint
#2010 • Original Price: $14.50
Issued: 1993 • Retired: 1994
Variation: no patches on left arm

① New!

	Value
NE	N/E

Caren B. Bearlove (GCC Exclusive)
#227722GCC • Original Price: N/A
Issued: 1999 • To Be Retired: 1999

②

	Values
1E	$350
2E	$238
3E	$180
AE	$63

Celeste... The Angel Rabbit
#2230 • Original Price: $16.50
Issued: 1994 • Retired: 1997

③

	Values
1E	$127
2E	$90
3E	$75
AE	$57

Charlotte & Bebe... The Gardeners
#2229 • Original Price: $16
Issued: 1994 • Retired: 1995

④

	Values (U.S.)
1E	$72
2E	$55
3E	$43
AE	$35

**Chelsea Kainada... The Practice
(LE-1997, Canadian Exclusive)**
#BC22851 • Original Price: $29.99 (Can.)
Issued: 1997 • Retired: 1997

⑤ New!

	Values
1E	$17
2E	$17
3E	$17
AE	$17

Chrissie... Game, Set, Match
#227717 • Original Price: $17
Issued: 1999 • Current

GENERAL FIGURINES

	Date Purchased	Price Paid	Value Of My Collection
1.			
2.			
3.			
4.			
5.			
✎ PENCIL TOTALS			

①

Values	
1E	$147
2E	$98
3E	$82
AE	$45

Christian By The Sea

#2012 • Original Price: $14.50
Issued: 1993 • Retired: 1998

②

Values (U.S.)	
1E	$950
2E	N/A
3E	N/A
AE	N/A

Christmas Bear Elf With List (LE-1,872, Canadian Exclusive)

#BC2051 • Original Price: $24.99 (Can.)
Issued: 1994 • Retired: 1994

③

Values	
1E	N/A
2E	N/A
3E	N/A
AE	$25
Variation	
1E	$435
2E	$275
3E	$230
AE	$40

Clara ... The Nurse (RS)

#2231 • Original Price: $16
Issued: 1994 • Retired: 1998
Variation: original version

④

Values	
1E	$140
2E	$97
3E	$82
AE	$60

Clarence Angel Bear

#2029-11 • Original Price: $13
Issued: 1994 • Retired: 1995

GENERAL FIGURINES

	Date Purchased	Price Paid	Value Of My Collection
1.			
2.			
3.			
4.			
5.			
PENCIL TOTALS			

⑤

Values	
1E	$30
2E	$21
3E	$21
AE	$21
Variation 1	
NE	$45
Variation 2	
1E	$42
2E	$33
3E	$25
AE	$21

The Collector (RS)

#227707 • Original Price: $21
Issued: 1998 • Current
Variation 1: 1997 GCC Early Release;
Variation 2: original version

①

Values	
1E	$82
2E	$62
3E	$55
AE	$36

Cookie Catberg...Knittin' Kitten
#2250 • Original Price: $19
Issued: 1995 • Retired: 1997

②

Values	
1E	$100
2E	$72
3E	$64
AE	$50

Cookie The Santa Cat
#2237 • Original Price: $15.50
Issued: 1994 • Retired: 1995

③

Values	
1E	$95
2E	$63
3E	$49
AE	$18

Daphne & Eloise...Women's Work
#2251 • Original Price: $18
Issued: 1995 • To Be Retired: 12/31/99

④

Values	
1E	$152
2E	$110
3E	$83
AE	$56

Daphne Hare & Maisey Ewe
#2011 • Original Price: $14.50
Issued: 1993 • Retired: 1995

⑤

Values	
1E	$146
2E	$98
3E	$77
AE	$32

Daphne...The Reader Hare
#2226 • Original Price: $14.50
Issued: 1994 • Retired: 1998

GENERAL FIGURINES

	Date Purchased	Price Paid	Value Of My Collection
1.			
2.			
3.			
4.			
5.			
PENCIL TOTALS			

①

Value

NE $36

Dean Newbearger III ... Bears & Bulls (GCC Exclusive)
#227715GCC • Original Price: $16
Issued: 1998 • Retired: 1998

②

Values

1E	$44
2E	$36
3E	$27
AE	$15

Dr. Harrison Griz ... M.D., Ph.D., B.U.D.
#228309 • Original Price: $15
Issued: 1998 • Current

③

Values

1E	$85
2E	$48
3E	$35
AE	$14

Eddie ... Proud To Be A Bearmerican

#228312 • Original Price: $14
Issued: 1998 • Current

④

Values

1E	$185
2E	$102
3E	$76
AE	$24

Edmund & Bailey ... Gathering Holly
#2240 • Original Price: $24
Issued: 1994 • Current

GENERAL FIGURINES

	Date Purchased	Price Paid	Value Of My Collection
1.			
2.			
3.			
4.			
5.			
PENCIL TOTALS			

⑤

Values

1E	$45
2E	$37
3E	$29
AE	$15

Edmund The Elf ... The Christmas Carol
#228311 • Original Price: $15
Issued: 1998 • Current

①

Values	
1E	$29
2E	$17
3E	$17
AE	$17
Variation	
1E	$55
2E	$40
3E	$28
AE	$17

Edmund … The Graduate
– Carpe Diem (RS)
#227701-07 • Original Price: $17
Issued: 1997 • Current
Variation: original version

②

Values	
1E	$108
2E	$82
3E	$59
AE	$51

Elgin The Elf Bear
#2236 • Original Price: $14.50
Issued: 1994 • Retired: 1997

③

Value	
NE	$53

Elizabeth … I Am The Queen
(LE-1998, Special Event Piece)
#01998-71 • Original Price: $35
Issued: 1998 • Retired: 1998

④

Values	
1E	$110
2E	$84
3E	$68
AE	$15.50

Elliot & Snowbeary
#2242 • Original Price: $15.50
Issued: 1994 • Current

⑤

Values	
1E	$258
2E	$150
3E	$112
AE	$16.50

Elliot & The Tree
#2241 • Original Price: $16.50
Issued: 1994 • Current

GENERAL FIGURINES

	Date Purchased	Price Paid	Value Of My Collection
1.			
2.			
3.			
4.			
5.			
PENCIL TOTALS			

①

Values

1E	$92
2E	$65
3E	$48
AE	$17

Elliot ... The Hero
#2280 • Original Price: $17
Issued: 1996 • Current

②

Values

1E	$60
2E	$39
3E	$30
AE	$19

Elvira & Chauncey Fitzbruin ...
Shipmates
#227708 • Original Price: $19
Issued: 1998 • Current

③

Values

1E	$88
2E	$66
3E	$52
AE	$18

Emma & Bailey ... Afternoon Tea
#2277 • Original Price: $18
Issued: 1996 • To Be Retired: 12/31/99

④

Values

1E	$78
2E	$57
3E	$46
AE	$17.50

Emma ... The Witchy Bear
#2269 • Original Price: $17.50
Issued: 1995 • Current

GENERAL FIGURINES

	Date Purchased	Price Paid	Value Of My Collection
1.			
2.	28E/2017 99	Gift	
3.			
4.			
5.			
✏ PENCIL TOTALS			

⑤

Value (U.S.)

NE $68

Ewell & Walton ...
Manitoba Mooselmen
(LE-12,000, Canadian Exclusive)
#BC2228 • Original Price: $24.99 (Can.)
Issued: 1996 • Retired: 1997

①

Values	
1E	$495
2E	N/A
3E	N/A
AE	N/A

Father Chrisbear And Son
#2008 • Original Price: $14.50
Issued: 1993 • Retired: 1993

②

Values	
1E	$58
2E	$40
3E	$29
AE	$20

Feldman D. Finklebearg And Dooley ... "Painless And The Patient"
#227710 • Original Price: $20
Issued: 1998 • Current

③ New!

Values	
1E	$34
2E	$34
3E	$34
AE	$34

Flash McBear & The Sitting
#227721 • Original Price: $34
Issued: 1999 • Current

④

Values	
JAN	$95
FEB	$86
MAR	$80
APR-DEC	$72

The Flying Lesson... This End Up (LE-1997)
#227801 • Original Price: $63
Issued: 1997 • Retired: 1997

⑤ New!

Values	
JAN	$48
FEB	$48
MAR	$48
APR-DEC	$48

Gary, Tina, Matt & Bailey... From Our Home To Yours (LE-1999)
#227804 • Original Price: $48
Issued: 1999 • To Be Retired: 1999

GENERAL FIGURINES

	Date Purchased	Price Paid	Value Of My Collection
1.			
2.			
3.			
4.			
5.			
✎ PENCIL TOTALS			

(1)

Values	
1E	$68
2E	$53
3E	$38
AE	$19

Grace & Jonathan ... Born To Shop
#228306 • Original Price: $19
Issued: 1997 • Current

(2)

Values	
1E	N/A
2E	$125
3E	$98
AE	$26
Variation	
1E	$425
2E	N/A
3E	N/A
AE	N/A

Grenville & Beatrice ... Best Friends
#2016 • Original Price: $26
Issued: 1994 • To Be Retired: 12/31/99
Variation: dove on right front stones

(3)

Values	
1E	$120
2E	$92
3E	$70
AE	$37

Grenville & Beatrice ... True Love
#2274 • Original Price: $37
Issued: 1996 • Current

(4)

Values	
1E	$80
2E	$62
3E	$54
AE	$28

Grenville & Knute ... Football Buddies
#2255 • Original Price: $20
Issued: 1995 • Retired: 1998

GENERAL FIGURINES

	Date Purchased	Price Paid	Value Of My Collection
1.			
2.			
3.			
4.			
5.			
PENCIL TOTALS			

(5)

Value	
NE	$23
Variation	
NE	$150

Grenville & Neville ... The Sign
#2099 • Original Price: $16
Issued: 1993 • Retired: 1998
Variation: brown bottom

①

Values	
1E	$132
2E	$88
3E	$78
AE	$60

Grenville ... The Graduate
#2233 • Original Price: $16.50
Issued: 1994 • Retired: 1996

②

Values	
1E	$540
2E	$355
3E	$310
AE	$195

Grenville The Santabear
#2030 • Original Price: $14.50
Issued: 1994 • Retired: 1996

③

Values	
JAN	$150
FEB	$97
MAR	$83
APR-DEC	$68

**Grenville ... The Storyteller
(LE-1995)**
#2265 • Original Price: $47
Issued: 1995 • Retired: 1995

④

Values	
1E	$620
2E	$495
3E	N/A
AE	N/A

Grenville ... With Green Scarf
#2003-04 • Original Price: $11
Issued: 1993 • Retired: 1993

⑤

Values	
1E	$87
2E	$65
3E	$53
AE	$36

**Grenville With Matthew &
Bailey ... Sunday Afternoon**
#2281 • Original Price: $36
Issued: 1996 • Current

GENERAL FIGURINES

	Date Purchased	Price Paid	Value Of My Collection
1.			
2.			
3.			
4.			
5.			
PENCIL TOTALS			

1

Values	
1E	N/A
2E	N/A
3E	N/A
AE	$64
Variation	
1E	$165
2E	$105
3E	$88
AE	$64

Grenville...With Red Scarf (RS)
#2003-08 • Original Price: $11
Issued: 1993 • Retired: 1995
Variation: original version

2

Values	
1E	$50
2E	$34
3E	$25
AE	$15

Guinevere The Angel... Love Is The Master Key
#228308 • Original Price: $15
Issued: 1998 • Current

3

Value	
PR	$80

Gwain & Guinevere (set/2, QVC Premier Edition)
N/A • Original Price: N/A
Issued: 1997 • Retired: 1997

4

Values	
1E	$105
2E	$60
3E	$44
AE	$16

Homer On The Plate
#2225 • Original Price: $16
Issued: 1994 • To Be Retired: 12/31/99

GENERAL FIGURINES

	Date Purchased	Price Paid	Value Of My Collection
1.			
2.			
3.			
4.			
5.			
PENCIL TOTALS			

5

Values (U.S.)	
1E	$98
2E	$75
3E	$52
AE	$25

Homer On The Plate (Canadian Exclusive)
#BC2210 • Original Price: $24.99 (Can.)
Issued: 1994 • Current

①

Value	
NE	$38

Honey B. Elfberg With Gabriella
(Parade Of Gifts Exclusive)
#94577POG • Original Price: $18.50
Issued: 1998 • Retired: 1998

②

Values	
1E	$78
2E	$57
3E	$45
AE	$14

Hop-A-Long…The Deputy
#2247 • Original Price: $14
Issued: 1995 • Current

③

Values	
1E	$24
2E	$12
3E	$12
AE	$12
Variation	
1E	$60
2E	$46
3E	$37
AE	$12

Humboldt…The Simple Bear (RS)
#227703 • Original Price: $12
Issued: 1997 • Current
Variation: original version

④

Values	
1E	$34
2E	$29
3E	$23
AE	$20
Variation	
1E	$65
2E	$44
3E	$38
AE	$24

Judge Griz…Hissonah (RS)
#228303 • Original Price: $18.50
Issued: 1997 • Retired: 1998
Variation: original version

⑤

Values	
1E	$140
2E	$92
3E	$75
AE	$63

Juliette Angel Bear
#2029-10 • Original Price: $13
Issued: 1994 • Retired: 1995

GENERAL FIGURINES

	Date Purchased	Price Paid	Value Of My Collection
1.			
2.			
3.			
4.			
5.			
PENCIL TOTALS			

①

Values	
1E	$135
2E	$89
3E	$75
AE	$26

Justina & M. Harrison ... Sweetie Pies
#2015 • Original Price: $26
Issued: 1994 • To Be Retired: 12/31/99

②

Values	
1E	$67
2E	$47
3E	$38
AE	$16

Justina ... The Message "Bearer"
#2273 • Original Price: $16
Issued: 1996 • Current

③

Values	
1E	$95
2E	$78
3E	$64
AE	$44

Knute & The Gridiron
#2245 • Original Price: $16.50
Issued: 1994 • Retired: 1997

④

Values	
1E	$110
2E	$79
3E	$66
AE	$14.50

Kringle & Bailey With List
#2235 • Original Price: $14.50
Issued: 1994 • To Be Retired: 12/31/99

GENERAL FIGURINES

	Date Purchased	Price Paid	Value Of My Collection
1.			
2.			
3.			
4.			
5.			
PENCIL TOTALS			

⑤

Values	
1E	$85
2E	$64
3E	$50
AE	$18

Kringle And Company
#2283 • Original Price: $18
Issued: 1996 • Current

①

Values
1E $120
2E $77
3E $67
AE $49

Kringle And Company (GCC Exclusive)
#2283-01 • Original Price: $18
Issued: 1996 • Retired: 1996

②

Values
1E $95
2E $55
3E $46
AE $15

Lefty On The Mound
#2253 • Original Price: $15
Issued: 1995 • Current

③

Values (U.S.)
1E $100
2E $70
3E $53
AE $30

Lefty On The Mound (Canadian Exclusive)
#BC2066 • Original Price: $24.99 (Can.)
Issued: 1994 • Current

④

Values
1E $32
2E $19
3E $19
AE $19
Variation
1E $67
2E $46
3E $30
AE $19

Louella & Hedda … The Secret (RS)
#227705 • Original Price: $19
Issued: 1997 • Current
Variation: original version

⑤

Values (U.S.)
1E $175
2E $130
3E $95
AE $76

Lucy Big Pig, Little Pig (Canadian Exclusive)
#BC2050 • Original Price: $24.99 (Can.)
Issued: 1994 • Retired: 1996

GENERAL FIGURINES

	Date Purchased	Price Paid	Value Of My Collection
1.			
2.			
3.			
4.			
5.			
PENCIL TOTALS			

1

Values	
1E	$67
2E	$53
3E	$35
AE	$17

M. Harrison's Birthday
#2275 • Original Price: $17
Issued: 1996 • To Be Retired: 12/31/99

2

Values	
1E	$95
2E	$68
3E	$58
AE	$15.50

Manheim The Eco-Moose
#2243 • Original Price: $15.50
Issued: 1994 • Current

3

Values	
PR	$75
1E	$52
2E	$43
3E	$34
AE	$18

Margot ... The Ballerina
#227709 • Original Price: $18
Issued: 1998 • Current

4

Values	
1E	$115
2E	$88
3E	$72
AE	$47

Maynard The Santa Moose
#2238 • Original Price: $15.50
Issued: 1994 • Retired: 1997

GENERAL FIGURINES

	Date Purchased	Price Paid	Value Of My Collection
1.			
2.			
3.			
4.			
5.			
PENCIL TOTALS			

5

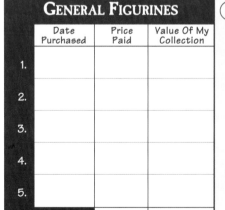

Values	
1E	$58
2E	$46
3E	$32
AE	$15

Momma McBear & Caledonia ... Quiet Time
#227711 • Original Price: $15
Issued: 1998 • Current

(1)

Values	
1E	$75
2E	$45
3E	$33
AE	$15

Momma McBear... Anticipation
#2282 • Original Price: $15
Issued: 1996 • Current

(2)

Values	
1E	N/A
2E	N/A
3E	N/A
AE	$90
Variation	
1E	$210
2E	$140
3E	$110
AE	$98

Moriarty — The Bear In The Cat Suit
#2005 • Original Price: $14
Issued: 1993 • Retired: 1995
Variation: 1993 on side of base

(3)

Values	
1E	$165
2E	$98
3E	$74
AE	$18.50

Ms. Bruin & Bailey... The Lesson
#2259 • Original Price: $18.50
Issued: 1995 • Current

(4)

Values	
1E	$100
2E	$72
3E	$55
AE	$35
Variation	
1E	$122
2E	$95
3E	$76
AE	$64

Ms. Griz... Monday Morning
#2276 • Original Price: $35
Issued: 1996 • To Be Retired: 12/31/99
Variation: pink dress

(5)

Values	
1E	$58
2E	$42
3E	$30
AE	$15
Variation	
1E	$82
2E	$54
3E	$42
AE	$33

Ms. Griz... Saturday Night
#2284 • Original Price: $15
Issued: 1997 • Current
Variation: 1996 GCC Early Release

GENERAL FIGURINES

	Date Purchased	Price Paid	Value Of My Collection
1.			
2.			
3.			
4.			
5.			
PENCIL TOTALS			

①

Values
1E	$30
2E	$16.50
3E	$16.50
AE	$16.50

Variation
1E	$62
2E	$40
3E	$27
AE	$16.50

Neville... Compubear (RS)
#227702 • Original Price: $16.50
Issued: 1997 • Current
Variation: original version

②

Values
1E	$140
2E	$100
3E	$80
AE	$62

Neville... The Bedtime Bear
#2002 • Original Price: $14.50
Issued: 1993 • Retired: 1996

③

Values
JAN	$185
FEB	$130
MAR	$115
APR-DEC	$98

Noah & Co... Ark Builders (LE-1996)
#2278 • Original Price: $63
Issued: 1996 • Retired: 1996

④

Values
1E	$92
2E	$72
3E	$64
AE	$57

Otis... Tax Time
#2262 • Original Price: $19
Issued: 1995 • Retired: 1997

GENERAL FIGURINES

	Date Purchased	Price Paid	Value Of My Collection
1.			
2.			
3.			
4.			
5.			
PENCIL TOTALS			

⑤

Values
1E	$82
2E	$58
3E	$44
AE	$28

Otis... The Fisherman
#2249-06 • Original Price: $16
Issued: 1995 • Retired: 1998

①

Value
NE $60

Prince Hamalot
(Special Event Piece, LE-1997)
#01997-71 • Original Price: $30
Issued: 1997 • Retired: 1997

②

Values
1E $54
2E $39
3E $29
AE $18.50

Puck ... Slapshot
#228305 • Original Price: $18.50
Issued: 1997 • Current

③

Values
1E $55
2E $46
3E $32
AE $19

Rocky Bruin ... Score, Score, Score
#228307 • Original Price: $19
Issued: 1998 • Current

④

Values
1E $60
2E $47
3E $35
AE $25

S.C. Northstar & Emmett ...
Lil' Helper
#228310 • Original Price: $25
Issued: 1998 • Current

⑤

Values
1E $117
2E $82
3E $65
AE $56

Sebastian's Prayer
#2227 • Original Price: $16.50
Issued: 1994 • Retired: 1996

GENERAL FIGURINES

	Date Purchased	Price Paid	Value Of My Collection
1.			
2.			
3.			
4.			
5.			
✏ PENCIL TOTALS			

① Values

1E	$160
2E	$108
3E	$80
AE	$60

Sherlock & Watson ... In Disguise
#2019 • Original Price: $16
Issued: 1994 • Retired: 1996

② Values

1E	$76
2E	$55
3E	$42
AE	$26

Simone & Bailey ... Helping Hands
#2267 • Original Price: $26
Issued: 1995 • Current

③ Values

1E	N/A
2E	N/A
3E	N/A
AE	$100

Variation

1E	$365
2E	$210
3E	$160
AE	$120

Simone de Bearvoire & Her Mom, My Auntie Alice
#2001 • Original Price: $14.50
Issued: 1993 • Retired: 1996
Variation: no patches on paws

④ Values

1E	$88
2E	$60
3E	$45
AE	$21

Sir Edmund ... Persistence
#2279 • Original Price: $21
Issued: 1996 • To Be Retired: 12/31/99

GENERAL FIGURINES

	Date Purchased	Price Paid	Value Of My Collection
1.			
2.			
3.			
4.			
5.			
PENCIL TOTALS			

⑤ Value

PR $55

Sparky And The Box (QVC Premier Edition)
N/A • Original Price: $20
Issued: 1998 • Retired: 1998

1

Values	
1E	$56
2E	$44
3E	$33
AE	$19

Stonewall ... The Rebel
#228302 • Original Price: $19
Issued: 1997 • Current

2

Values	
1E	$160
2E	$112
3E	$84
AE	$52

Ted & Teddy
#2223 • Original Price: $16
Issued: 1994 • Retired: 1997

3

Values	
JAN	$100
FEB	$82
MAR	$75
APR-DEC	$68

T.H.B. & Co ... Work Is Love Made Visible (LE-1998)
#227803 • Original Price: $63
Issued: 1998 • Retired: 1998

4

Value	
NE	N/E

Uncle Gus & Gary ... The Gift
(sold as set with "Uncle Gus" & "Honey Bunch" *Mohair Bears*, QVC Exclusive)
N/A • Original Price: $106
Issued: 1997 • Retired: 1997

5

Values	
1E	$88
2E	$60
3E	$46
AE	$35

Union Jack ... Love Letters
#2263 • Original Price: $19
Issued: 1995 • Retired: 1998

GENERAL FIGURINES

	Date Purchased	Price Paid	Value Of My Collection
1.			
2.			
3.			
4.			
5.			
✏ PENCIL TOTALS			

① New!

Value
NE $26

Victoria Regina Buzzbruin...
So Many Flowers, So Little Time
(Special Event Piece, LE-1999)
#01999-71 • Original Price: $26
Issued: 1999 • To Be Retired: 1999

②

Values
1E $285
2E $210
3E $150
AE $18.50

Victoria... The Lady
#2004 • Original Price: $18.50
Issued: 1993 • To Be Retired: 12/31/99

③ New!

Values
1E $18
2E $18
3E $18
AE $18

Wanda & Gert...
A Little Off The Top
#227719 • Original Price: $18
Issued: 1999 • Current

④

Values
1E $155
2E $105
3E $85
AE $54

Wilson At The Beach
#2020-06 • Original Price: $16
Issued: 1994 • Retired: 1997

GENERAL FIGURINES

	Date Purchased	Price Paid	Value Of My Collection
1.			
2.	35E/2/42 99	Gift	
3.			
4.			
5.			
✏ PENCIL TOTALS			

⑤

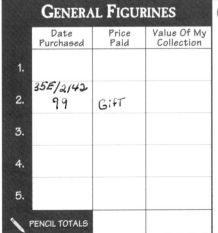

Values
1E $125
2E $94
3E $67
AE $42

Wilson The Perfesser
#2222 • Original Price: $16.50
Issued: 1994 • Retired: 1997

①

Values	
1E	$82
2E	$57
3E	$45
AE	$16.50

Wilson...The Wonderful Wizard Of Wuz
#2261 • Original Price: $16.50
Issued: 1995 • Current

②

Values	
1E	$575
2E	$430
3E	$300
AE	$65

Wilson With Love Sonnets
#2007 • Original Price: $13
Issued: 1993 • Retired: 1997

③

Value	
NE	$52

Zoe... The Angel Of Life (GCC Exclusive)
#2286 • Original Price: $14
Issued: 1997 • Retired: 1997

HOLIDAY PAGEANT SERIES

In 1995, the curtain opened on this pageant with 3 bears portraying Mary, Joseph and The Child in a manger, as well as a stage backdrop. Each subsequent year featured the introduction of four new pieces and December 31, 1999 will be the final curtain call as the entire series of pageant thespians will be honored with the status of retirement.

④

Values	
1E	$53
2E	$35
3E	$25
AE	$15

Ariel & Clarence... As The Pair O' Angels
#2411 • Original Price: $15
Issued: 1997 • To Be Retired: 12/31/99

GENERAL FIGURINES

	Date Purchased	Price Paid	Value Of My Collection
1.			
2.			
3.			

HOLIDAY PAGEANT SERIES

4.			
PENCIL TOTALS			

(1)

Values	
1E	$60
2E	$44
3E	$30
AE	$15

Baldwin... As The Child
#2403 • Original Price: $15
Issued: 1995 • To Be Retired: 12/31/99

(2)

Values	
1E	$49
2E	$38
3E	$27
AE	$15

Bruce... As The Shepherd
#2410 • Original Price: $15
Issued: 1997 • To Be Retired: 12/31/99

(3)

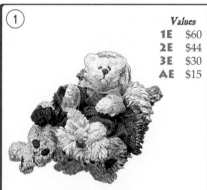

Values	
1E	$45
2E	$33
3E	$26
AE	$16

Caledonia... As The Narrator
#2412 • Original Price: $16
Issued: 1998 • To Be Retired: 12/31/99

(4)

Values	
1E	$50
2E	$33
3E	$25
AE	$15

Essex... As The Donkey
#2408 • Original Price: $15
Issued: 1997 • To Be Retired: 12/31/99

HOLIDAY PAGEANT SERIES

	Date Purchased	Price Paid	Value Of My Collection
1.			
2.			
3.			
4.			
5.			
PENCIL TOTALS			

(5)

Values	
1E	$56
2E	$42
3E	$28
AE	$15

Heath... As Caspar
#2405 • Original Price: $15
Issued: 1996 • To Be Retired: 12/31/99

BEARSTONES

① Matthew … As The Drummer

Values	
1E	$50
2E	$40
3E	$29
AE	$16

#2415 • Original Price: $16
Issued: 1998 • To Be Retired: 12/31/99

② Ms. Bruin … As The Teacher

Values	
1E	$46
2E	$37
3E	$27
AE	$16

#2414 • Original Price: $16
Issued: 1998 • To Be Retired: 12/31/99

③ Neville … As Joseph

Values	
1E	$59
2E	$40
3E	$26
AE	$15

#2401 • Original Price: $15
Issued: 1995 • To Be Retired: 12/31/99

④ Raleigh … As Balthasar

Values	
1E	$57
2E	$43
3E	$30
AE	$15

#2406 • Original Price: $15
Issued: 1996 • To Be Retired: 12/31/99

⑤ Serendipity … As The Guardian Angel

Values	
1E	$47
2E	$37
3E	$28
AE	$16

#2416 • Original Price: $16
Issued: 1998 • To Be Retired: 12/31/99

HOLIDAY PAGEANT SERIES

	Date Purchased	Price Paid	Value Of My Collection
1.			
2.			
3.			
4.			
5.			
PENCIL TOTALS			

①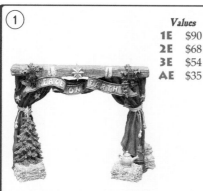

	Values
1E	$90
2E	$68
3E	$54
AE	$35

The Stage...School Pageant
#2425 • Original Price: $35
Issued: 1995 • To Be Retired: 12/31/99

②

	Values
1E	$62
2E	$42
3E	$29
AE	$18

Thatcher & Eden...As The Camel
#2407 • Original Price: $18
Issued: 1996 • To Be Retired: 12/31/99

③

	Values
1E	$62
2E	$45
3E	$28
AE	$15

Theresa...As Mary
#2402 • Original Price: $15
Issued: 1995 • To Be Retired: 12/31/99

④

	Values
1E	$55
2E	$41
3E	$27
AE	$15

Wilson...As Melchior
#2404 • Original Price: $15
Issued: 1996 • To Be Retired: 12/31/99

HOLIDAY PAGEANT SERIES

	Date Purchased	Price Paid	Value Of My Collection
1.			
2.			
3.			
4.			
5.			
✏ PENCIL TOTALS			

⑤

	Values
1E	$45
2E	$27
3E	$20
AE	$12

Winkie & Dink...As The Lambs
#2409 • Original Price: $12
Issued: 1997 • To Be Retired: 12/31/99

NOAH'S PAGEANT SERIES

This year marks the debut of a brand new series of promising young actors, illustrating the saga of Noah and his famous boat, the Ark. Boyds is promising the addition of four pieces per year until the final act in 2002. The four introductions in 1999 include Noah, his wife, a pair of giraffe sentinels and the Ark, itself.

① New!

Values	
1E	$11
2E	$11
3E	$11
AE	$11

Bernice As Mrs. Noah ... Chief Cook

#2427 • Original Price: $11
Issued: 1999 • Current

② New!

Values	
1E	$11
2E	$11
3E	$11
AE	$11

Jeremy As Noah ... The Ark Builder

#2426 • Original Price: $11
Issued: 1999 • Current

③ New!

Values	
1E	$36
2E	$36
3E	$36
AE	$36

S. S. Noah ... The Ark

#2450 • Original Price: $36
Issued: 1999 • Current

④ New!

Values	
1E	$11
2E	$11
3E	$11
AE	$11

Stretch & Skye ... The Lookouts

#2428 • Original Price: $11
Issued: 1999 • Current

NOAH'S PAGEANT SERIES

	Date Purchased	Price Paid	Value Of My Collection
1.			
2.			
3.			
4.			
PENCIL TOTALS			

OTHER BEARSTONE COLLECTIBLES

The Bearstone Collection also offers a variety of other pieces spilling into every facet of life. These pieces include a clock, seven frames, three musicals, two wall sconces, 25 ornaments, an ornament stand, three GCC exclusive plaques, 12 votive holders, nine waterglobes and 26 San Francisco Music Boxes.

①

Values	
1E	$85
2E	$70
3E	$45
AE	$37

Bailey ... On Time
#27600 • Original Price: $37
Issued: 1997 • To Be Retired: 12/31/99

② New!

Values	
1E	$24
2E	$24
3E	$24
AE	$24

Bailey ... Life Is A Daring Adventure
#27354 • Original Price: $24
Issued: 1999 • Current

③

Values	
1E	$53
2E	$32
3E	$28
AE	$24

Bailey ... "True Love"
#27351 • Original Price: $24
Issued: 1998 • Current

CLOCKS

	Date Purchased	Price Paid	Value Of My Collection
1.			

FRAMES

2.			
3.			
4.			
✎ PENCIL TOTALS			

④

Values	
PR	$65
1E	$55
2E	$32
3E	$28
AE	$24
Variation	
NE	$55

The Collector
#27301 • Original Price: $24
Issued: 1998 • Current
Variation: 1997 GCC Early Release "The Masterpiece"

BEARSTONES

①

Values	
PR	$68
1E	$65
2E	$32
3E	$28
AE	$24

Edmund...
The Night Before Christmas
#27302 • Original Price: $24
Issued: 1998 • Current

② New!

Values	
1E	$24
2E	$24
3E	$24
AE	$24

Rocky... All Star
#27353 • Original Price: $24
Issued: 1999 • Current

③

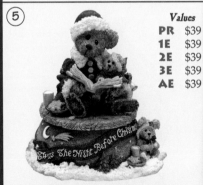

Values	
1E	$50
2E	$30
3E	$27
AE	$23

Wilson... Life Is But A Dream
#27350 • Original Price: $23
Issued: 1998 • Current

④

Values	
JAN	$48
FEB	$37
MAR	$32
APR-DEC	$27

Wings To Soar (LE-1997)
#27300 • Original Price: $23
Issued: 1997 • Retired: 1997

⑤

Values	
PR	$39
1E	$39
2E	$39
3E	$39
AE	$39

Bailey... The Night Before Christmas
#270501 • Original Price: $39
Issued: 1998 • Current

FRAMES

	Date Purchased	Price Paid	Value Of My Collection
1.			
2.			
3.			
4.			

MUSICALS

5.			
PENCIL TOTALS			

① New!

Values	
1E	$36
2E	$36
3E	$36
AE	$36

Daphne And Eloise... Women's Work
#270553 • Original Price: $36
Issued: 1999 • Current

② New!

Values	
1E	$39
2E	$39
3E	$39
AE	$39

Ms. Bruin & Bailey ... The Lesson
#270554 • Original Price: $39
Issued: 1999 • Current

③

Values	
1E	$25
2E	$10
3E	$10
AE	$10

Above The Clouds (ornament stand)
#25990 • Original Price: $10
Issued: 1997 • Current

④

Value	
NE	$22

Baby's Christmas "1998" (LE-1998)
#25954 • Original Price: $13
Issued: 1998 • Retired: 1998

MUSICALS

	Date Purchased	Price Paid	Value Of My Collection
1.			
2.			

ORNAMENTS

3.			
4.			
5.			
PENCIL TOTALS			

⑤

Value	
NE	$30

Baby's First Christmas (NALED Exclusive)
#25703 • Original Price: $12
Issued: 1997 • Retired: 1997

BEARSTONES

①

Values	
1E	$25
2E	$11
3E	$11
AE	$11

Bailey … Home Sweet Home
#25708 • Original Price: $11
Issued: 1998 • Current

②

Value	
NE	$10

Celestina … Peace Angel
#25710 • Original Price: $10
Issued: 1998 • Current

③

Value	
NE	$36

Charity … Angel Bear With Star
#2502 • Original Price: $10
Issued: 1994 • Retired: 1996

④

Values	
1E	$28
2E	$24
3E	$20
AE	$15

Clair With Gingerbread Man
#25701 • Original Price: $11
Issued: 1996 • Retired: 1998

⑤

Value	
NE	$32

Edmund … "Believe"
#2505 • Original Price: $10
Issued: 1995 • Retired: 1997

ORNAMENTS

	Date Purchased	Price Paid	Value Of My Collection
1.			
2.			
3.			
4.			
5.			
✏ PENCIL TOTALS			

①

Values	
1E	$28
2E	$24
3E	$20
AE	$15

Edmund With Wreath
#25700 • Original Price: $11
Issued: 1996 • Retired: 1998

②

Value	
NE	$32

Elliot With Tree
#2507 • Original Price: $10
Issued: 1995 • Retired: 1997

③

Value	
NE	$40

Faith... Angel Bear With Trumpet
#2500 • Original Price: $10
Issued: 1994 • Retired: 1996

④

Values	
1E	$25
2E	$11
3E	$11
AE	$11

George And Gracie... Forever
#25707 • Original Price: $11
Issued: 1998 • Current

ORNAMENTS

	Date Purchased	Price Paid	Value Of My Collection
1.			
2.			
3.			
4.			
5.			
✐ PENCIL TOTALS			

⑤

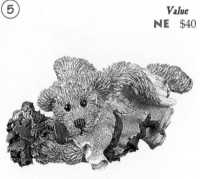

Value	
NE	$40

Hope... Angel Bear With Wreath
#2501 • Original Price: $10
Issued: 1994 • Retired: 1996

①

Value
NE $10

Juliette... Love Angel
#25712 • Original Price: $10
Issued: 1998 • Current

②

Values
1E $24
2E $11
3E $11
AE $11

Knute... Half Time
#25705 • Original Price: $11
Issued: 1998 • Current

③

Values
1E $24
2E $11
3E $11
AE $11

Larry... Nuthin' But Net
#25706 • Original Price: $11
Issued: 1998 • Current

④

Value
NE $32

Manheim The Moose With Wreath
#2506 • Original Price: $10
Issued: 1995 • Retired: 1997

⑤

Value
NE $24

Matthew With Kip...
Baby's First Christmas "1997"
#2508 • Original Price: $10
Issued: 1997 • Retired: 1997

ORNAMENTS

	Date Purchased	Price Paid	Value Of My Collection
1.			
2.			
3.			
4.			
5.			
✏ PENCIL TOTALS			

① **Value**
NE $26

McKenzie … Shootin' Star
(GCC Exclusive)
#25952GCC • Original Price: $21.50
Issued: 1998 • Retired: 1998

② **Value**
NE $29

Noel Bruinski …
Da Electrician "1998" (LE-1998)
#25953 • Original Price: $13
Issued: 1998 • Retired: 1998

③ **Values**
1E $34
2E $11
3E $11
AE $11

Regina D. Ferrisdaval …
I Am The Queen
#25709 • Original Price: $11
Issued: 1998 • Current

④ **Values**
1E $24
2E $11
3E $11
AE $11

Rocky … Score, Score, Score
#25704 • Original Price: $11
Issued: 1998 • Current

ORNAMENTS

	Date Purchased	Price Paid	Value Of My Collection
1.			
2.			
3.			
4.			
5.			
PENCIL TOTALS			

⑤ **Value**
NE $10

Serena … Joy Angel
#25711 • Original Price: $10
Issued: 1998 • Current

① *Value*
NE $28

Serendipity...
"Peace" To All (LE-1998)
#25955 • Original Price: $21
Issued: 1998 • Retired: 1998

② *Values*
1E $28
2E $24
3E $20
AE $15

Wilson With Shooting Star
#25702 • Original Price: $11
Issued: 1996 • Retired: 1998

③ *Value*
NE $55

Zoe...Starlight Christmas
(GCC Exclusive)
#25951GCC • Original Price: $21.50
Issued: 1997 • Retired: 1997

④ *Value*
NE $34

Angelica...In Flight
(GCC Exclusive)
#654282GCC • Original Price: $19.50
Issued: 1998 • Retired: 1998

⑤ *Value*
NE $39

Edmund...Deck The Halls
(GCC Exclusive)
#65428GCC • Original Price: $19.50
Issued: 1997 • Retired: 1997

ORNAMENTS

	Date Purchased	Price Paid	Value Of My Collection
1.			
2.			
3.			

PLAQUES

4.			
5.			
✏ PENCIL TOTALS			

①

	Value
NE	$36

Elliot The Hero (GCC Exclusive)
#654281GCC • Original Price: $20
Issued: 1998 • Retired: 1998

②

	Values
1E	$38
2E	$21
3E	$21
AE	$21

Clarence & Raphael ... Angels Fly High
#654291 • Original Price: $21
Issued: 1998 • Current

③

	Values
1E	$43
2E	$16
3E	$16
AE	$16

Heavenly Wall Sconce
#65429 • Original Price: $16
Issued: 1997 • Retired: 1998

④

	Values
1E	$50
2E	$27
3E	$27
AE	$27

Bailey & Huck ... Wheee!!!
#27752 • Original Price: $27
Issued: 1998 • Current

PLAQUES

	Date Purchased	Price Paid	Value Of My Collection
1.			

SCONCES

2.			
3.			

VOTIVE HOLDERS

4.			
5.			
✏ PENCIL TOTALS			

⑤

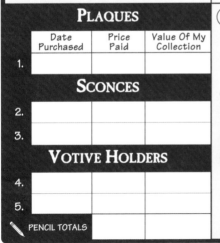

	Values
1E	$45
2E	$25
3E	$25
AE	$25

Bailey & Matthew ... The Gift
#27723 • Original Price: $25
Issued: 1998 • Current

①

Values	
1E	$52
2E	$28
3E	$28
AE	$28

**Clarence & Angelica...
Flight Training**
#27722 • Original Price: $28
Issued: 1998 • Current

②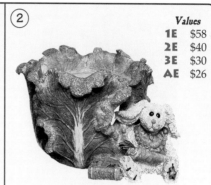

Values	
1E	$58
2E	$40
3E	$30
AE	$26

Daphne... In The Cabbage Patch
#27750 • Original Price: $26
Issued: 1997 • To Be Retired: 12/31/99

③

Values	
1E	$73
2E	$58
3E	$45
AE	$26

**Edmund The Elf Bear...
Holiday Glow**
#2772 • Original Price: $26
Issued: 1996 • Retired: 1998

④

Values	
1E	$73
2E	$58
3E	$45
AE	$26

**Elgin And Elliot The Elves...
Toasty Warm**
#2771 • Original Price: $26
Issued: 1996 • Current

⑤

Values	
1E	$73
2E	$58
3E	$45
AE	$26

**Emma The Witchy Bear...
Pumpkin Magic**
#2770 • Original Price: $26
Issued: 1996 • Retired: 1998

VOTIVE HOLDERS

	Date Purchased	Price Paid	Value Of My Collection
1.			
2.			
3.			
4.			
5.			
PENCIL TOTALS			

①

Values	
1E	$60
2E	$44
3E	$35
AE	$26

M. Harrison...
The Ambush At Birch Tree
#27721 • Original Price: $26
Issued: 1997 • Current

②

Values	
1E	$58
2E	$40
3E	$32
AE	$26

Maynard & Melvin...
Tales Of The North
#27720 • Original Price: $26
Issued: 1997 • Current

③

Values	
1E	$26
2E	$26
3E	$26
AE	$26
Variation	
1E	$60
2E	$40
3E	$32
AE	$26

Ms. Bruin & Bailey ... Tea Time (RS)
#27751 • Original Price: $26
Issued: 1997 • Current
Variation: original version

④ New!

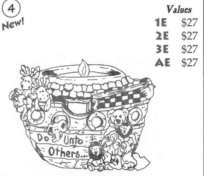

Values	
1E	$27
2E	$27
3E	$27
AE	$27

Noah ... And The Golden Rule
#27754 • Original Price: $27
Issued: 1999 • Current

VOTIVE HOLDERS

	Date Purchased	Price Paid	Value Of My Collection
1.			
2.			
3.			
4.			
5.			
✏ PENCIL TOTALS			

⑤

Values	
1E	$53
2E	$27
3E	$27
AE	$27

Sebastian & Nicholas...
The Lost Ball
#27753 • Original Price: $27
Issued: 1998 • To Be Retired: 12/31/99

①

Value
NE $68

Angelica ... The Guardian
#2702 • Original Price: $38
Issued: 1995 • Retired: 1998

②

Values
1E $66
2E $60
3E $55
AE $51
Variation
1E $80
2E $60
3E $55
AE $51

The Collector
#270551 • Original Price: $51
Issued: 1998 • Current
Variation: 1997 GCC Early Release

③

Value
NE $88

Elliot & The Tree
#2704 • Original Price: $36
Issued: 1995 • Retired: 1997

④ **New!**

Values
1E $38
2E $38
3E $38
AE $38

Elvira & Chauncey ... Shipmates
#270552 • Original Price: $38
Issued: 1999 • Current

⑤

Value
NE $135

**The Flying Lesson ...
This End Up (LE-10,000)**
#270601 • Original Price: $63
Issued: 1997 • Retired: 1997

WATERGLOBES

	Date Purchased	Price Paid	Value Of My Collection
1.			
2.			
3.			
4.			
5.			
✏ PENCIL TOTALS			

(1)

	Value
NE	$76

Grenville The Santabear
#2700 • Original Price: $36
Issued: 1994 • Retired: 1996

(2)

	Values
1E	$70
2E	$58
3E	$52
AE	$36

Homer On The Plate
#270550 • Original Price: $36
Issued: 1997 • To Be Retired: 12/31/99

(3)

	Value
NE	$290

Noah & Co. (LE-1996)
#2706 • Original Price: $53
Issued: 1996 • Retired: 1996

(4)

	Values
1E	$70
2E	$52
3E	$45
AE	$36

Simone & Bailey ... Helping Hands
#2705 • Original Price: $36
Issued: 1996 • Retired: 1998

WATERGLOBES

	Date Purchased	Price Paid	Value Of My Collection
1.			
2.			
3.			
4.			

SAN FRANCISCO MUSIC BOXES

5.			

✏ PENCIL TOTALS

(5)

	Values
1E	$77
2E	$60
3E	$52
AE	$45

Amelia's Enterprise
♪ *The Impossible Dream*
#2759SF • Original Price: $45
Issued: 1997 • Retired: 1999

①

Values	
1E	$92
2E	$62
3E	$53
AE	$45
Variation	
1E	$167
2E	N/A
3E	N/A
AE	N/A

Arthur On Trunk
♪ *Let Me Be Your Teddy Bear*
#2751SF • Original Price: $40
Issued: 1995 • Retired: 1997
Variation: bear and trunk larger,
painted bottom, paw print on scarf

②

Values	
1E	$90
2E	$70
3E	$56
AE	$45

Bailey & Emily
♪ *Teddy Bear's Picnic*
#2757SF • Original Price: $45
Issued: 1996 • Retired: 1999

③

Values	
1E	$78
2E	$45
3E	$45
AE	$45

Bailey Honey Bear
♪ *You Are The Sunshine Of My Life*
#2767SF • Original Price: $45
Issued: 1998 • Current

④

Values	
1E	$88
2E	$73
3E	$60
AE	$40

Bailey With Suitcase
♪ *Let Me Be Your Teddy Bear*
#2755SF • Original Price: $40
Issued: 1996 • Retired: 1999

⑤

Values	
1E	$75
2E	$45
3E	$45
AE	$45

Bailey's Birthday
♪ *Happy Birthday*
#2763SF • Original Price: $45
Issued: 1997 • Retired: 1999

SAN FRANCISCO MUSIC BOXES

	Date Purchased	Price Paid	Value Of My Collection
1.			
2.			
3.			
4.			
5.			
✏ PENCIL TOTALS			

①

Values
1E $70
2E $45
3E $45
AE $45

Born To Shop
♪ *We've Only Just Begun*
#2773SF • Original Price: $45
Issued: 1998 • Current

② New!

Values
1E $55
2E $55
3E $55
AE $55

Checkers
♪ *You Light Up My Life*
#2778SF • Original Price: $55
Issued: 1999 • Current

③ New!

Values
1E $45
2E $45
3E $45
AE $45

Clara The Nurse
♪ *A Spoonful Of Sugar*
#2777SF • Original Price: $45
Issued: 1999 • Current

④

Values
1E $85
2E $65
3E $52
AE $40

Clarence Angel
♪ *When You Wish Upon A Star*
#2753SF • Original Price: $40
Issued: 1996 • Retired: 1999

SAN FRANCISCO MUSIC BOXES

	Date Purchased	Price Paid	Value Of My Collection
1.			
2.			
3.			
4.			
5.			
PENCIL TOTALS			

⑤

Values
1E $78
2E $69
3E $56
AE $50

The Collector
♪ *My Favorite Things*
#2762SF • Original Price: $50
Issued: 1997 • Retired: 1999

①

Values	
1E	$82
2E	$63
3E	$52
AE	$45

Daphne And Eloise
♪ *You've Got A Friend*
#2251SF • Original Price: $45
Issued: 1997 • Retired: 1999

②

Values	
1E	$25
2E	$18
3E	$17
AE	$15

Deck The Halls (ornament)
♪ *Christmas medley*
#2765SF • Original Price: $15
Issued: 1997 • Current

③

Values	
1E	$95
2E	$72
3E	$56
AE	$45

Emma & Bailey Tea Party
♪ *Tea For Two*
#2752SF • Original Price: $45
Issued: 1996 • Retired: 1999

④

Values	
1E	$70
2E	$45
3E	$45
AE	$45

Grenville & Beatrice
♪ *Mendelssohn's "Wedding March"*
#2770SF • Original Price: $45
Issued: 1998 • Current

⑤

Values	
1E	$73
2E	$45
3E	$45
AE	$45

Heart's Desire
♪ *Let Me Call You Sweetheart*
#2772SF • Original Price: $45
Issued: 1998 • Current

SAN FRANCISCO MUSIC BOXES

	Date Purchased	Price Paid	Value Of My Collection
1.			
2.			
3.			
4.			
5.			
PENCIL TOTALS			

①

Values	
1E	$77
2E	$58
3E	$52
AE	$45

Homer On The Plate
♪ *Take Me Out To The Ballgame*
#2761SF • Original Price: $45
Issued: 1997 • Retired: 1999

②

Values	
1E	$70
2E	$45
3E	$45
AE	$45

Justina Message Bearer
♪ *I'll Have To Say I Love You*
In A Song
#2769SF • Original Price: $45
Issued: 1998 • Current

③

Values	
1E	$78
2E	$50
3E	$50
AE	$50

Kringle & Co.
♪ *Have Yourself A Merry*
Little Christmas
#27745SF • Original Price: $50
Issued: 1998 • Current

④

Values	
1E	$89
2E	$70
3E	$64
AE	$45

Miss Bruin & Bailey
♪ *Getting To Know You*
#2756SF • Original Price: $45
Issued: 1996 • Retired: 1999

SAN FRANCISCO MUSIC BOXES

	Date Purchased	Price Paid	Value Of My Collection
1.			
2.			
3.			
4.			
5.			
✏ PENCIL TOTALS			

⑤

Values	
1E	$85
2E	$66
3E	$57
AE	$40

Neville Bedtime
♪ *A Dream Is A Wish Your*
Heart Makes
#2754SF • Original Price: $40
Issued: 1996 • Retired: 1999

①

Values	
1E	$68
2E	$45
3E	$45
AE	$45

Neville Compubear
♪ *Nine To Five*
#2768SF • Original Price: $45
Issued: 1998 • Current

②

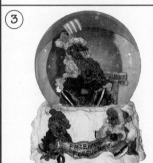

Values	
1E	$79
2E	$62
3E	$55
AE	$50

The Secret
♪ *That's What Friends Are For*
#2764SF • Original Price: $50
Issued: 1997 • Retired: 1999

③

Values	
1E	$90
2E	$64
3E	$52
AE	$45

Simone & Bailey
♪ *song title unavailable*
#2758SF • Original Price: $45
Issued: 1996 • Retired: 1996

④

Values	
1E	$92
2E	$72
3E	$55
AE	$47
Variation	
1E	$155
2E	$140
3E	$130
AE	N/A

Ted & Teddy
♪ *For The Good Times*
#2701SF • Original Price: $45
Issued: 1995 • Retired: 1997
Variation: bears and crate slightly larger

⑤

Values	
1E	$88
2E	$70
3E	$59
AE	$50
Variation	
1E	$155
2E	$140
3E	$125
AE	N/A

Wilson With Love Sonnets
♪ *You're Nobody Till Somebody Loves You*
#2750SF • Original Price: $40
Issued: 1995 • Retired: 1997
*Variation: book base is larger,
large folds in sweater*

SAN FRANCISCO MUSIC BOXES

	Date Purchased	Price Paid	Value Of My Collection
1.			
2.			
3.			
4.			
5.			
✏ PENCIL TOTALS			

BEARWEAR PINS

For the fashion-conscious, or those who just want to wear their love for Boyds on their lapel, there are 17 new pins for the spring season. With 83 designs to choose from, featuring a variety of themes from hobbies to professions to special events, there is a piece of Bearwear for everyone.

①

Alden & Priscilla...
The Pilgrims
Issued: 1995 • Retired
#2635 • *Value: $10*

②

Alden...Trick Or Treat
Issued: 1998 • Current
#26022 • *Value: $4*

③
New!

Alice Spillen...Waitressing
Issued: 1999 • Current
#26123 • *Value: $4*

④

Alice's Flight
Issued: 1995 • Retired
#2616 • *Value: $10*

⑤

Amelia
Issued: 1995 • Retired
#2612 • *Value: $10*

⑥

Angelica With Lily
Issued: 1995 • Retired
#2663 • *Value: $12*

BEARWEAR PINS

	Price Paid	Value Of My Collection
1.		
2.		
3.		
4.		
5.		
6.		
7.		
8.		
9.		
10.		
11.	Gift *unnumbered*	
12.		
13.		
14.		
15.		
16.		
17.		
18.		
PENCIL TOTALS		

⑦

Angelica's Flight
Issued: 1994 • Retired
#2605 • *Value: $12*

⑧

Ariel...Love Conquers All
Issued: 1998 • Current
#26019 • *Value: $4*

⑨

Arlo In The
Pumpkin Wreath
Issued: 1997 • Retired
#26012 • *Value: $12*

⑩
New!

Arnold...Chip N' Putt
Issued: 1999 • Current
#26121 • *Value: $4*

⑪

Bailey & Becky...
Diary Secrets
Issued: 1998 • Current
#26107 • *Value: $4*

⑫

Bailey & Emma...
The Sisters
Issued: 1995 • Retired
#2634 • *Value: $10*

⑬
New!

Bailey...Birthday Wishes
Issued: 1999 • Current
#26117 • *Value: $4*

⑭

Bailey...Born To Shop
Issued: 1998 • Current
#26016 • *Value: $4*

⑮
New!

Bailey...Carpe Diem
Issued: 1999 • Current
#26118 • *Value: $4*

⑯

Bailey...Chocolate Wreath
Issued: 1997 • Retired
#26104 • *Value: $10*

⑰

Bailey In Spring Bonnet
Issued: 1995 • Retired
#2667 • *Value: $12*

⑱

Bailey In The Garden
Issued: 1998 • Current
#26105 • *Value: $4*

Value Guide — The Bearstone Collection®

1

**Bailey...Life Is
A Daring Adventure**
Issued: 1998 • Current
#26106 • *Value: $4*

2

Bailey...Love Conquers All
Issued: 1998 • Current
#26108 • *Value: $4*

3

Bailey...Tea Time
Issued: 1997 • Retired
#26102 • *Value: $10*

4

Bailey...The Graduate
Issued: 1998 • Current
#26109 • *Value: $4*

5

Bailey's Bonnet
Issued: 1994 • Retired
#2608 • *Value: $16*

6

Bailey's Garden
Issued: 1995 • Retired
#2615 • *Value: $10*

7

Bailey's Springtime
Issued: 1995 • Retired
#2617 • *Value: $10*

8

Bessie's Chris-moo-se
Issued: 1994 • Retired
#2604 • *Value: $12*

9
New!

Chrissie...Tennis Anyone?
Issued: 1999 • Current
#26122 • *Value: $4*

10

Clara...Get Well
Issued: 1997 • Current
#26103 • *Value: $4*

11
New!

**Daffodil...
The Colors Of Sunshine**
Issued: 1999 • Current
#26127 • *Value: $4*

BEARWEAR PINS

	Price Paid	Value Of My Collection
1.		
2.		
3.		
4.		
5.		
6.		
7.		
8.		
9.		
10.		
11.		
12.		
13.		
14.		
15.		
16.		
17.		
18.		
19.		
20.		

12
New!

**Dahlia...
My Biggest Blossom**
Issued: 1999 • Current
#26126 • *Value: $4*

13

Daphne With Dove
Issued: 1995 • Retired
#2611 • *Value: $9*

14

**Edmund And
Bailey...Caroling**
Issued: 1996 • Retired
#26003 • *Value: $10*

15

Edmund...Deck The Halls
Issued: 1998 • Current
#26021 • *Value: $4*

16

**Edmund The Santa
Bear...Believe**
Issued: 1996 • Retired
#26004 • *Value: $10*

17

Elgin The Elf Bear
Issued: 1995 • Retired
#2631 • *Value: $10*
*Variation: brown fur
trim on hat
Value: N/E*

18

Elliot And The Lights
Issued: 1995 • Retired
#2642 • *Value: $10*

19

**Elliot Bear With
Jingle Bell Wreath**
Issued: 1995 • Retired
#2636 • *Value: $12*

20

Elliot...The Fireman
Issued: 1996 • Retired
#26001 • *Value: $9*

PENCIL TOTALS

Elliot With Tree
Issued: 1996 • Retired
#26002 • *Value:* $10

Elliot's Wreath
Issued: 1994 • Retired
#2606 • *Value:* $12

Emma The Witchy Bear
Issued: 1995 • Retired
#2632 • *Value:* $9

Ernest On The Pumpkin Wreath
Issued: 1996 • Retired
#26005 • *Value:* $12

Felicity...Stocking Stuffer
Issued: 1998 • Current
#26015 • *Value:* $4

Flash McBear
Issued: 1999 • Current
#26115 • *Value:* $4

Grace...Born To Shop
Issued: 1997
To Be Retired
#26010 • *Value:* $4

Grenville...The "Flakie" Santa Bear
Issued: 1997 • Retired
#26009 • *Value:* $8

BEARWEAR PINS

	Price Paid	Value Of My Collection
1.		
2.		
3.		
4.		
5.		
6.		
7.		
8.		
9.		
10.		
11.		
12.		
13.		
14.		
15.		
16.		
17.		
18.		
19.		
20.		
PENCIL TOTALS		

Heather...Hugs And Kisses
Issued: 1998 • Current
#26112 • *Value:* $4

Homer
Issued: 1995 • Retired
#2618 • *Value:* $10

Iris...Purple Passion
Issued: 1999 • Current
#26128 • *Value:* $4

J.B. & The Basketballs
Issued: 1997 • Retired
#26100 • *Value:* $9

Juliette With Rose
Issued: 1995 • Retired
#2662 • *Value:* $12

Justina, Bailey & M.Harrison
Issued: 1995 • Retired
#2619 • *Value:* $10

Kringle & Northrop The Pup
Issued: 1997 • Retired
#26008 • *Value:* $9

M. Harrison
Issued: 1994 • Retired
#2601 • *Value:* $12

Mabel Goodheart...Practice Random Acts Of Kindness
Issued: 1998 • Current
#26110 • *Value:* $4

Margot... Dance Dance Dance
Issued: 1998 • Current
#26114 • *Value:* $4

McKenzie...Shootin' Star
Issued: 1997 • Retired
#26006 • *Value:* $8

Milo...Up, Up, And Away
Issued: 1999 • Current
#26116 • *Value:* $4

BEARSTONES

1. Mistress Bailey
Issued: 1995 • Retired
#2614 • *Value:* $12

2. New! Momma...Anticipation
Issued: 1999 • Current
#26120 • *Value:* $4

3. Ms. Bruin...Learn!
Issued: 1998
To Be Retired
#26111 • *Value:* $4

4. Murgatroyd The Chrismoose
Issued: 1994 • Retired
#2603 • *Value:* $27

5. Nicholas
Issued: 1994 • Retired
#2600 • *Value:* $12

6. Punkin Puss
Issued: 1997 • Retired
#26014 • *Value:* $9

7. The Queen
(Special Event Pin)
Issued: 1998 • Retired
#01998-81 • *Value:* $12

8. New! Queen Bee
(Special Event Pin)
Issued: 1999
To Be Retired
N/A • *Value:* $4

9. New! Rocky...Goal Kick
Issued: 1999 • Current
#26119 • *Value:* $4

10. New! Rose...Garden Classics
Issued: 1999 • Current
#26129 • *Value:* $4

11. S. C. Northstar...
Ho! Ho! Ho!
Issued: 1998 • Current
#26017 • *Value:* $4

12. Santa Cat
Issued: 1994 • Retired
#2607 • *Value:* $14

13. Shelley's Flight
Issued: 1995 • Retired
#2639 • *Value:* $10

14. Simone In Heart Wreath
Issued: 1995 • Retired
#2679 • *Value:* $10

15. Snowbeary &
The Snowflakes
Issued: 1997 • Retired
#26007 • *Value:* $9

16. New! Snowy...
The First Sign Of Spring
Issued: 1999 • Current
#26124 • *Value:* $4

17. Springtime Bessie
Issued: 1995 • Retired
#2610 • *Value:* $10

18. Stella...Believe In Angels
Issued: 1998 • Current
#26018 • *Value:* $4

19. New! Tulip...
An Armful Of Blooms
Issued: 1999 • Current
#26125 • *Value:* $4

20. Wilson...Hugs & Kisses
Issued: 1997
To Be Retired
#26011 • *Value:* $4

BEARWEAR PINS

	Price Paid	Value Of My Collection
1.		
2.		
3.		
4.		
5.		
6.		
7.		
8.		
9.		
10.		
11.		
12.		
13.		
14.		
15.		
16.		
17.		
18.		
19.		
20.		
	PENCIL TOTALS	

①	②	③	④

Wilson... In Love	**Wilson The Wizard... Boo!**	**Wilson With Love Sonnets**	**Wilson's Flight**
Issued: 1997 • Retired	Issued: 1998 • Current	Issued: 1998 • Current	Issued: 1994 • Retired
#26101 • *Value:* **$9**	#26023 • *Value:* **$4**	#26020 • *Value:* **$4**	#2609 • *Value:* **$15**

⑤

New!

*photo
not
available*

1999 Canadian Exclusive Pin
Issued: 1999 • Current
#BC94281 • *Value:* **N/A**

EXCLUSIVE PIN SETS

When not walking the collectibles runway, these pins enjoyed the exclusive spotlight on QVC. Sold in sets of three, these pieces mirror the antics of their Bearstone and Folkstone figurine counterparts and are often very difficult to pin down, even though many of the sets were offered on several shows over a period of years.

BEARWEAR PINS

	Price Paid	Value Of My Collection
1.		
2.		
3.		
4.		
5.		
6.		
7.		
8.		
9.		

PENCIL TOTALS

⑥

Amelia The Bunny, Bailey With Blue Bow & Bailey With Straw Hat (set/3)
Issued: 1996 • Retired
N/A • *Value:* **N/E**

⑦

Amelia The Bunny, Bailey With Blue Bow & Hop-A-Long (set/3)
Issued: 1995 • Retired
N/A • *Value:* **N/E**

⑧

Angelica The Angel, Bessie The Cow & Emma In Spring Bonnet (set/3)
Issued: 1996 • Retired
N/A • *Value:* **N/E**

⑨

Beatrice The Giftgiver, Clarence The Angel & Jingles The Snowman (set/3)
Issued: 1995 • Retired
N/A • *Value:* **N/E**

GENERAL FIGURINES

In a whimsical flashback to the folk-art days of the Boyds Collection Ltd., these tall and lanky angels and animals honor a variety of professions and offer a bit of guidance from the heavens above. The introduction of eight new pieces to the line bring the total number of pieces in the collection to 97. And with themes ranging from bowling to waitressing, there is a bit of this rustic appeal to offer just about anyone.

①

Values	
1E	$44
2E	$35
3E	$27
AE	$23
Variation	
1E	$62
2E	$45
3E	$32
AE	$28

Abigail ... Peaceable Kingdom (GRS)
#2829 • Original Price: $19
Issued: 1995 • Retired: 1998
Variation: original version

②

Values	
1E	$58
2E	$45
3E	$35
AE	$30

Alvin T. MacBarker ... Dog Face
#2872 • Original Price: $19
Issued: 1996 • Retired: 1997

③

Values	
1E	$53
2E	$42
3E	$38
AE	$32
Variation	
1E	$80
2E	$66
3E	$53
AE	$39

Angel Of Freedom (GRS)
#2820 • Original Price: $16
Issued: 1994 • Retired: 1996
Variation: original version

④

Values	
1E	$59
2E	$46
3E	$37
AE	$33
Variation	
1E	$92
2E	$68
3E	$58
AE	$42

Angel Of Love (GRS)
#2821 • Original Price: $16
Issued: 1994 • Retired: 1996
Variation: original version

GENERAL FIGURINES

	Date Purchased	Price Paid	Value Of My Collection
1.			
2.			
3.			
4.			
PENCIL TOTALS			

① Angel Of Peace (GRS)

Values	
1E	$54
2E	$42
3E	$37
AE	$28
Variation	
1E	$88
2E	$69
3E	$48
AE	$35

#2822 • Original Price: $16
Issued: 1994 • Retired: 1997
Variation: original version

② Astrid Isinglass… Snow Angel (LE-1997)

Value	
NE	$80

#28206-06 • Original Price: $23
Issued: 1997 • Retired: 1997

③ Athena… The Wedding Angel

Values	
1E	$56
2E	$39
3E	$27
AE	$19

#28202 • Original Price: $19
Issued: 1996 • Current

④ Audubon P. Pussywillow… The Birdwatcher

New!

Values	
1E	$19
2E	$19
3E	$19
AE	$19

#2868 • Original Price: $19
Issued: 1999 • Current

General Figurines

	Date Purchased	Price Paid	Value Of My Collection
1.			
2.			
3.			
4.			
PENCIL TOTALS			

①

Values	
PR	$60
1E	$52
2E	$32
3E	$24
AE	$20

Auntie Cocoa M. Maximus...
Chocolate Angel
#28242 • Original Price: $20
Issued: 1998 • Current

②

Values	
1E	$43
2E	$30
3E	$25
AE	$19.50

Bearly Nick And Buddies
#28001 • Original Price: $19.50
Issued: 1997 • Current

③

Values	
1E	$52
2E	$35
3E	$27
AE	$23
Variation 1 & 2	
1E	$60
2E	$46
3E	$33
AE	$24

Beatrice... The Birthday Angel (GRS)
#2825 • Original Price: $19
Issued: 1995 • Retired: 1998
Variation 1: writing on bow hard to read;
Variation 2: taller

④

Values	
1E	$55
2E	$40
3E	$36
AE	$18

Beatrice... The Giftgiver
#2836 • Original Price: $18
Issued: 1995 • To Be Retired: 12/31/99

⑤

Values	
1E	$48
2E	$32
3E	$25
AE	$18

Bernie... Igotwatiwanted
St. Bernard Santa
#2873 • Original Price: $18
Issued: 1996 • Current

GENERAL FIGURINES

	Date Purchased	Price Paid	Value Of My Collection
1.			
2.			
3.			
4.			
5.			
	PENCIL TOTALS		

①

	Values
1E	N/A
2E	N/A
3E	N/A
AE	$19
	Variation
1E	$84
2E	$62
3E	$46
AE	$40

Betty Biscuit
#2870 • Original Price: $19
Issued: 1996 • Current
Variation: "Betty Cocker"

②

	Values
1E	$43
2E	$32
3E	$24
AE	$20

Birdie Holeinone...
NQGA Of Golfers
#28245 • Original Price: $20
Issued: 1998 • Current

③

	Values
1E	$50
2E	$34
3E	$27
AE	$18
	Variation
1E	$59
2E	$48
3E	$36
AE	$28

Boowinkle Von Hindenmoose (GRS)
#2831 • Original Price: $18
Issued: 1995 • Current
Variation: original version

④

	Value
NE	$44

Bristol... Just Sweepin'
(Catalog Exclusive)
#28101 • Original Price: $17
Issued: 1997 • Retired: 1997

GENERAL FIGURINES

	Date Purchased	Price Paid	Value Of My Collection
1.			
2.			
3.			
4.			
5.			
✏ PENCIL TOTALS			

⑤

	Values
1E	$55
2E	$39
3E	$30
AE	$19

Buster Goes a' Courtin'
#2844 • Original Price: $19
Issued: 1996 • Current

①

Values	
1E	$87
2E	$64
3E	$50
AE	$33

Chilly & Son With Dove
#2811 • Original Price: $16
Issued: 1994 • Retired: 1997

②

Value	
NE	$92

**Constance & Felicity ...
Best Friend Angels (LE-1997)**
#28205 • Original Price: $38
Issued: 1997 • Retired: 1997

③

Values	
1E	$65
2E	$48
3E	$40
AE	$19

Cosmos ... The Gardening Angel
#28201 • Original Price: $19
Issued: 1996 • Current

④ New!

Values	
1E	$20
2E	$20
3E	$20
AE	$20

**Domestica T. Whirlwind ...
NQGA Of Super Moms**
#28249 • Original Price: $20
Issued: 1999 • Current

GENERAL FIGURINES

	Date Purchased	Price Paid	Value Of My Collection
1.			
2.			
3.			
4.			
✏ PENCIL TOTALS			

①

Values	
1E	$58
2E	$34
3E	$25
AE	$18

Egon...The Skier
#2837 • Original Price: $18
Issued: 1996 • To Be Retired: 12/31/99

②

Values	
1E	$58
2E	$36
3E	$26
AE	$18

Elmer...Been Farmin' Long?
#2851 • Original Price: $18
Issued: 1995 • Current

③

Values	
1E	$60
2E	$42
3E	$35
AE	$26

Elmo "Tex" Beefcake...
On The Range
#2853 • Original Price: $19
Issued: 1996 • Retired: 1997

④

Values	
1E	$63
2E	$43
3E	$30
AE	$18

Ernest Hemmingmoose...
The Hunter
#2835 • Original Price: $18
Issued: 1995 • To Be Retired: 12/31/99

GENERAL FIGURINES

	Date Purchased	Price Paid	Value Of My Collection
1.			
2.			
3.			
4.			
PENCIL TOTALS			

①

Values	
1E	$59
2E	$39
3E	$28
AE	$18

Esmeralda ... The Wonderful Witch
#2860 • Original Price: $18
Issued: 1995 • Current

②

Value	
NE	$172

Etheral ... Angel Of Light (LE-7,200)
#28203-06 • Original Price: $19
Issued: 1996 • Retired: 1996

③

Values	
1E	$55
2E	$35
3E	$26
AE	$21

Execunick ... The First
Global Business Man
#28002 • Original Price: $21
Issued: 1998 • Current

④

Values	
1E	$56
2E	$39
3E	$30
AE	$19

Flora, Amelia & Eloise ...
The Tea Party
#2846 • Original Price: $19
Issued: 1996 • To Be Retired: 12/31/99

⑤

Values	
1E	$58
2E	$39
3E	$28
AE	$19

Flora & Amelia ... The Gardeners
#2843 • Original Price: $19
Issued: 1996 • Current

GENERAL FIGURINES

	Date Purchased	Price Paid	Value Of My Collection
1.			
2.			
3.			
4.			
5.			
PENCIL TOTALS			

FOLKSTONES

①

Values	
1E	$52
2E	$43
3E	$35
AE	$32
Variation 1 & 2	
1E	$78
2E	$56
3E	$48
AE	$38

Florence ... The Kitchen Angel (GRS)
#2824 • Original Price: $19
Issued: 1995 • Retired: 1996
Variation 1: hand on bottom center of bowl;
Variation 2: longer skirt

②

Values	
PR	$55
1E	$46
2E	$35
3E	$27
AE	$20

Francoise & Suzanne ... The Spree
#2875 • Original Price: $20
Issued: 1998 • Current

③
New!

Values	
1E	$19
2E	$19
3E	$19
AE	$19

Harriet & Punch With Hermaine ...
The Challenge
#28402 • Original Price: $19
Issued: 1999 • Current

④

Values	
1E	$40
2E	$29
3E	$24
AE	$19

Helga With Ingrid & Anna ...
Be Warm
#2818 • Original Price: $19
Issued: 1997 • Current

GENERAL FIGURINES

	Date Purchased	Price Paid	Value Of My Collection
1.			
2.			
3.			
4.			
PENCIL TOTALS			

FOLKSTONES

①

Values	
1E	$53
2E	$38
3E	$26
AE	$20

I.B. Coldman... Ice Is Nice
#28102 • Original Price: $20
Issued: 1998 • Current

②

Values	
1E	$58
2E	$45
3E	$37
AE	$26

Ichabod Mooselman... The Pilgrim
#2833 • Original Price: $18
Issued: 1995 • Retired: 1997

③

Values	
1E	$38
2E	$24
3E	$22
AE	$18
Variation	
1E	$62
2E	$40
3E	$32
AE	$22

Ida & Bessie... The Gardeners (GRS)
#2852 • Original Price: $18
Issued: 1995 • Current
Variation: original version

④

Value	
NE	$46

Ike & Libby...
"Stars & Stripes Forever"
(Catalog Exclusive)
#281035SYN • Original Price: $20
Issued: 1998 • Retired: 1998

⑤

Values	
1E	$79
2E	$52
3E	$38
AE	$19

Illumina... Angel Of Light
#28203 • Original Price: $19
Issued: 1996 • To Be Retired: 12/31/99

GENERAL FIGURINES

	Date Purchased	Price Paid	Value Of My Collection
1.			
2.			
3.			
4.			
5.			
✏ PENCIL TOTALS			

①

Values	
1E	$37
2E	$21
3E	$19
AE	$17
Variation	
1E	$54
2E	$28
3E	$23
AE	$19

Jean Claude & Jacque ... The Skiers (GRS)

#2815 • Original Price: $17
Issued: 1995 • Current
Variation: original version

②

Values	
1E	$95
2E	$56
3E	$38
AE	$33

Jill ... Language Of Love

#2842 • Original Price: $18
Issued: 1995 • Retired: 1997

③

Values	
1E	$75
2E	$58
3E	$52
AE	$44
Variation	
1E	$110
2E	$77
3E	$63
AE	$58

Jingle Moose (GRS)

#2830 • Original Price: $16
Issued: 1994 • Retired: 1996
Variation: original version

④

Values	
1E	$100
2E	$65
3E	$52
AE	$46

Jingles & Son With Wreath

#2812 • Original Price: $16
Issued: 1994 • Retired: 1996

GENERAL FIGURINES

	Date Purchased	Price Paid	Value Of My Collection
1.			
2.			
3.			
4.			
PENCIL TOTALS			

FOLKSTONES

①

Values	
1E	$65
2E	$40
3E	$27
AE	$19

Krystal Isinglass ... Snow Angel
#28206 • Original Price: $19
Issued: 1997 • Current

② New!

Values	
1E	$18
2E	$18
3E	$18
AE	$18

Laverne B. Bowler ... Strikes & Spares
#28428 • Original Price: $18
Issued: 1999 • Current

③

Value	
NE	$95

Liddy Pearl ... How Does Your Garden Grow (LE-1998)
#2881 • Original Price: $40
Issued: 1998 • Retired: 1998

④

Values	
1E	$48
2E	$33
3E	$28
AE	$25
Variation 1 & 2	
1E	$63
2E	$46
3E	$38
AE	$33

Lizzie ... The Shopping Angel (GRS)
#2827 • Original Price: $19
Issued: 1995 • Retired: 1998
Variation 1: hand on strap 1/2" above purse;
Variation 2: many folds in skirt

⑤

Values	
1E	$52
2E	$33
3E	$26
AE	$19

**Loretta Moostein ...
"Yer Cheatin' Heart"**
#2854 • Original Price: $19
Issued: 1996 • To Be Retired: 12/31/99

General Figurines

	Date Purchased	Price Paid	Value Of My Collection
1.			
2.			
3.			
4.			
5.			
✏ PENCIL TOTALS			

1

Value
NE $60

Luminette ... By The Light Of The Silvery Moon (LE-1998)
#28207-06 • Original Price: $24
Issued: 1998 • Retired: 1998

2

Values
1E $45
2E $33
3E $25
AE $19

Luna ... By The Light Of The Silvery Moon
#28207 • Original Price: $19
Issued: 1998 • Current

3

Values
1E $47
2E $29
3E $25
AE $19

Madge ... The Magician/Beautician
#28243 • Original Price: $19
Issued: 1997 • Current

4

Values
1E $48
2E $32
3E $23
AE $19

Mercy ... Angel Of Nurses
#28240 • Original Price: $19
Issued: 1997 • Current

GENERAL FIGURINES

	Date Purchased	Price Paid	Value Of My Collection
1.			
2.			
3.			
4.			
PENCIL TOTALS			

FOLKSTONES

①

Values	
1E	$45
2E	$32
3E	$24
AE	$19

Miliken Von Hinden Moose...
Tree's Company
#2832 • Original Price: $19
Issued: 1998 • Current

②

Values	
1E	$50
2E	$35
3E	$28
AE	$24
Variation	
1E	$55
2E	$40
3E	$30
AE	$26

Minerva... The Baseball Angel
#2826 • Original Price: $19
Issued: 1995 • Retired: 1997
Variation: 6 buttons below belt

③

Values	
1E	$37
2E	$29
3E	$22
AE	$17.50

Miss Prudence... Multiplication
#2848 • Original Price: $17.50
Issued: 1998 • Current

④

Values	
1E	$50
2E	$34
3E	$25
AE	$19

Montague Von Hindenmoose...
Surprise!
#2839 • Original Price: $19
Issued: 1997 • Current

⑤ **New!**

Values	
1E	$19
2E	$19
3E	$19
AE	$19
Variation	
NE	$35

Ms. Fries...
Guardian Angel Of Waitresses
#28246 • Original Price: $19
Issued: 1999 • Current
Variation: 1998 GCC Early Release
"Ms. Fries . . . Not Quite The Guardian
Angel Of Waitresses"

GENERAL FIGURINES

	Date Purchased	Price Paid	Value Of My Collection
1.			
2.			
3.			
4.			
5.			
✏ PENCIL TOTALS			

1

Values
1E	$38
2E	$30
3E	$24
AE	$20

Variation
NE	$39

Ms. Imin Payne...
NOGA Of Exercisers
#28244 • Original Price: $20
Issued: 1998 • Current
Variation: 1998 GCC Early Release
"Iown Payne . . . Aerobics Angel"

2

New!

Values
1E	$20
2E	$20
3E	$20
AE	$20

Ms. McFrazzle...
Daycare Extraordinaire
#2883 • Original Price: $20
Issued: 1999 • Current

3

Values
1E	$60
2E	$38
3E	$30
AE	$23

Ms. Patience... Angel Of Teachers
#28241 • Original Price: $19
Issued: 1997 • Retired: 1998

4

New!

Values
1E	$21
2E	$21
3E	$21
AE	$21

Myron R. Fishmeister...
Angel Of Fish Stories
#28247 • Original Price: $21
Issued: 1999 • Current

GENERAL FIGURINES

	Date Purchased	Price Paid	Value Of My Collection
1.			
2.			
3.			
4.			
PENCIL TOTALS			

FOLKSTONES

①

	Values
1E	$62
2E	$38
3E	$28
AE	$24

Myrtle... Believe!
#2840 • Original Price: $18
Issued: 1995 • Retired: 1998

②

	Values
1E	$44
2E	$36
3E	$25
AE	$19

Nana McHare...
And The Love Gardeners
#2849 • Original Price: $19
Issued: 1998 • Current

③

	Value
NE	$160

Na-Nick And Siegfried...
The Plan (LE-10,000)
#2807 • Original Price: $34
Issued: 1996 • Retired: 1996

④

	Values
1E	$54
2E	$37
3E	$25
AE	$18
Variation	
1E	$66
2E	$45
3E	$37
AE	$23

Na-Nick Of The North (GRS)
#2804 • Original Price: $18
Issued: 1995 • Current
Variation: original version

⑤

	Values
1E	$52
2E	$30
3E	$23
AE	$18

Nanny... The Snowmom
#2817 • Original Price: $18
Issued: 1996 • Current

GENERAL FIGURINES

	Date Purchased	Price Paid	Value Of My Collection
1.			
2.			
3.			
4.			
5.			
✏ PENCIL TOTALS			

①

Values
1E	$105
2E	$63
3E	$42
AE	$32

Nicholai With Tree
#2800 • Original Price: $17
Issued: 1994 • Retired: 1997

②

Values
1E	$100
2E	$65
3E	$50
AE	$35

Nicholas With Book Of Lists
#2802 • Original Price: $17
Issued: 1994 • Retired: 1996

③

Values
1E	$52
2E	$36
3E	$28
AE	$18

Nicknoah ... Santa With Ark
#2806 • Original Price: $18
Issued: 1996 • Current

④

Values
1E	$88
2E	$55
3E	$38
AE	$29

Niki With Candle
#2801 • Original Price: $17
Issued: 1994 • Retired: 1997

GENERAL FIGURINES

	Date Purchased	Price Paid	Value Of My Collection
1.			
2.			
3.			
4.			
5.			
PENCIL TOTALS			

⑤

Values
1E	$60
2E	$43
3E	$35
AE	$24

No-No-Nick ... Bad Boy Santa
#2805 • Original Price: $18
Issued: 1996 • Retired: 1998

FOLKSTONES

①

Values	
1E	$50
2E	$38
3E	$30
AE	$24
Variation	
1E	$68
2E	$52
3E	$40
AE	$30

Northbound Willie (GRS)
#2814 • Original Price: $17
Issued: 1995 • Retired: 1997
Variation: original version

②

Values	
1E	$56
2E	$39
3E	$30
AE	$16
Variation	
1E	$100
2E	$62
3E	$42
AE	$28

Oceania ... Ocean Angel (GRS)
#2823 • Original Price: $16
Issued: 1995 • Retired: 1998
Variation: original version

③

Values	
1E	$48
2E	$32
3E	$24
AE	$16.50

Olaf ... Mogul Meister
#2819 • Original Price: $16.50
Issued: 1997 • Current

④

Values	
1E	$44
2E	$30
3E	$23
AE	$19

P. J. McSnoozin With Craxton ... Hibearnation
#2882 • Original Price: $19
Issued: 1998 • Current

⑤

Values	
1E	$40
2E	$28
3E	$23
AE	$20
Variation	
1E	$40
2E	$32
3E	$25
AE	$22

Peacenik ... The Sixties Santa
#2809 • Original Price: $20
Issued: 1998 • Current
Variation: 1997 GCC Early Release
"Peace-Nick"

GENERAL FIGURINES

	Date Purchased	Price Paid	Value Of My Collection
1.			
2.			
3.			
4.			
5.			
✏ PENCIL TOTALS			

①

Values
1E	$48
2E	$37
3E	$30
AE	$25

Variation
1E	$68
2E	$45
3E	$35
AE	$28

Peter ... The Whopper (GRS)
#2841 • Original Price: $18
Issued: 1995 • Retired: 1997
Variation: original version

②

Values
1E	$59
2E	$48
3E	$35
AE	$19

Polaris And The North Star ... On Ice
#2880 • Original Price: $19
Issued: 1997 • Current

③

Values
1E	$45
2E	$34
3E	$28
AE	$19

Prudence ... Daffodils
#2847 • Original Price: $19
Issued: 1997 • Current

④

Values
1E	$59
2E	$49
3E	$40
AE	$32

Prudence Mooselmaid ... The Pilgrim
#2834 • Original Price: $18
Issued: 1995 • Retired: 1997

GENERAL FIGURINES

	Date Purchased	Price Paid	Value Of My Collection
1.			
2.			
3.			
4.			
5.			
✏ PENCIL TOTALS			

⑤

Values
1E	$40
2E	$29
3E	$24
AE	$21

Purrscilla G. Pussenboots ... Mitten Knitters
#2865 • Original Price: $21
Issued: 1998 • Current

FOLKSTONES

1

Values	
1E	$43
2E	$31
3E	$22
AE	$19

Purrscilla... Give Thanks
#2866 • Original Price: $19
Issued: 1998 • Current

2

Values	
1E	$50
2E	$34
3E	$25
AE	$18

Robin... The Snowbird Lover
#2816 • Original Price: $18
Issued: 1996 • Current

3

Values	
1E	$40
2E	$28
3E	$25
AE	$18
Variation	
1E	$50
2E	$34
3E	$27
AE	$22

Rufus... Hoe Down (GRS)
#2850 • Original Price: $18
Issued: 1995 • To Be Retired: 12/31/99
Variation: original version

4

Values	
1E	$55
2E	$37
3E	$32
AE	$25
Variation	
1E	$57
2E	$45
3E	$33
AE	$25

St. Nick... The Quest
#2808 • Original Price: $20
Issued: 1996 • Retired: 1996
Variation: 1996 GCC Early Release

5

Value	
PR	$50

Salem... Give Thanks
(QVC Premier Edition)
N/A • Original Price: $19
Issued: 1998 • Retired: 1998

GENERAL FIGURINES

	Date Purchased	Price Paid	Value Of My Collection
1.			
2.			
3.			
4.			
5.			
✏ PENCIL TOTALS			

①

Values	
1E	$48
2E	$39
3E	$32
AE	$24
Variation	
1E	$68
2E	$47
3E	$37
AE	$30

Seraphina With Jacob & Rachael ... The Choir Angels (GRS)
#2828 • Original Price: $20
Issued: 1995 • Retired: 1997
Variation: original version

②

Values	
1E	$59
2E	$42
3E	$30
AE	$19

Serenity ... The Mother's Angel
#28204 • Original Price: $19
Issued: 1996 • Current

③

Values	
1E	$52
2E	$37
3E	$30
AE	$19.50

Sgt. Rex & Matt ... The Runaway
#2874 • Original Price: $19.50
Issued: 1997 • Current

④

Values	
1E	$45
2E	$33
3E	$25
AE	$17
Variation	
1E	$65
2E	$46
3E	$32
AE	$22

Siegfried & Egon ... The Sign (GRS)
#2899 • Original Price: $17
Issued: 1995 • Retired: 1998
Variation: original version

GENERAL FIGURINES

	Date Purchased	Price Paid	Value Of My Collection
1.			
2.			
3.			
4.			
5.			
✎ PENCIL TOTALS			

⑤

Values	
1E	$46
2E	$36
3E	$27
AE	$22
Variation	
1E	$64
2E	$42
3E	$35
AE	$28

Sliknick ... The Chimney Sweep (GRS)
#2803 • Original Price: $18
Issued: 1995 • Retired: 1998
Variation: original version

FOLKSTONES

①

	Values
1E	$56
2E	$42
3E	$30
AE	$19

Sparky McPlug
#2871 • Original Price: $19
Issued: 1996 • Current

②

	Values
1E	$50
2E	$36
3E	$28
AE	$19

"Too Loose" Lapin... "The Arte-e-st"
#2845 • Original Price: $19
Issued: 1996 • To Be Retired: 12/31/99

③
New!

	Values
1E	$20
2E	$20
3E	$20
AE	$20

**Wendy Willowhare...
A Tisket A Tasket**
#28401 • Original Price: $20
Issued: 1999 • Current

④

	Values
1E	$102
2E	$78
3E	$63
AE	$48

Windy With Book
#2810 • Original Price: $16
Issued: 1994 • Retired: 1996

⑤

	Values
1E	$48
2E	$32
3E	$27
AE	$19

Ziggy... The Duffer
#2838 • Original Price: $19
Issued: 1997 • To Be Retired: 12/31/99

GENERAL FIGURINES

	Date Purchased	Price Paid	Value Of My Collection
1.			
2.			
3.			
4.			
5.			
PENCIL TOTALS			

CARVERS CHOICE

The 1998 debut of these figurines inspired by folk art was a flashback of sorts to the wooden duck decoys and ornaments of the earliest days of The Boyds Collection Ltd. Larger than their Folkstone cousins, these pieces made a big impression among collectors and sold out quickly. In response to their popularity, Boyds released the next wave of smaller, open edition Carvers Choice figurines, with five new characters for 1999.

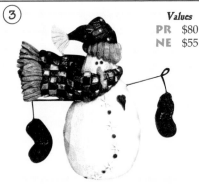

Values
PR $85
NE $63

Barnaby ... Homeward Bound (LE-18,000)
#370001 • Original Price: $38
Issued: 1998 • Retired: 1998

Values
1E $32
2E $19
3E $19
AE $19

Barnaby Jr ... Homeward Bound
#370101 • Original Price: $19
Issued: 1998 • Current

Values
PR $80
NE $55

Burt ... Bundle Up (LE-18,000)
#370002 • Original Price: $20
Issued: 1998 • Retired: 1998

CARVERS CHOICE

	Date Purchased	Price Paid	Value Of My Collection
1.			
2.			
3.			
4.			
PENCIL TOTALS			

Values
1E $30
2E $14
3E $14
AE $14

Burt Jr ... Bundle Up
#370102 • Original Price: $14
Issued: 1998 • Current

① **New!**

Values	
PR	$27
1E	$27
2E	$27
3E	$27
AE	$27

Chester Bigheart ... Love Much (LE-12,000)
#370053 • Original Price: $27
Issued: 1999 • Current

② **New!**

Values	
PR	$27
1E	$27
2E	$27
3E	$27
AE	$27

Jester Q. Funnybones ... Laugh Often
#370054 • Original Price: $27
Issued: 1999 • Current

③ **New!**

Values	
1E	$31
2E	$31
3E	$31
AE	$31

Lady Harriet Rushmore ... Never Enough Time
#370050 • Original Price: $31
Issued: 1999 • Current

④

Values	
PR	$100
NE	$80

Santa ... And The Final Inspection (LE-18,000)
#370003 • Original Price: $53
Issued: 1998 • Retired: 1998

⑤

Values	
1E	$35
2E	$24
3E	$24
AE	$24

Santa Jr ... And The Final Inspection
#370103 • Original Price: $24
Issued: 1998 • Current

CARVERS CHOICE

	Date Purchased	Price Paid	Value Of My Collection
1.			
2.			
3.			
4.			
5.			
PENCIL TOTALS			

FOLKSTONES

①

Values
PR $100
NE $80

Santa... In The Nick Of Time (LE-18,000)
#370000 • Original Price: $48
Issued: 1998 • Retired: 1998

②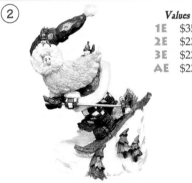

Values
1E $35
2E $23
3E $23
AE $23

Santa Jr... In The Nick Of Time
#370100 • Original Price: $23
Issued: 1998 • Current

③

Values
PR $100
NE $80

Santa... Quick As A Flash (LE-18,000)
#370004 • Original Price: $42
Issued: 1998 • Retired: 1998

④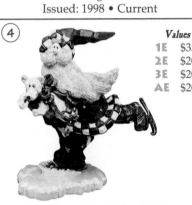

Values
1E $35
2E $20
3E $20
AE $20

Santa Jr... Quick As A Flash
#370104 • Original Price: $20
Issued: 1998 • Current

CARVERS CHOICE

	Date Purchased	Price Paid	Value Of My Collection
1.			
2.			
3.			
4.			
5.			
✎ PENCIL TOTALS			

⑤ New!

Values
1E $31
2E $31
3E $31
AE $31

Sir Simon Steadfast... Always Enough Time
#370051 • Original Price: $31
Issued: 1999 • Current

FOLKSTONES

① New!

Values	
PR	$27
1E	$27
2E	$27
3E	$27
AE	$27

Walter T. Goodlife...Live Well
#370052 • Original Price: $27
Issued: 1999 • Current

SANTA & FRIENDS

With the introduction of the jolly characters of Santa & Friends, The Folkstone Collection got a bit of Christmas spirit. In 1994, three of these five highly detailed Santas were issued, with the fourth and fifth pieces making their debut in 1996. By 1997, these hard-working characters were honored with retirement, passing on their festive responsibilities to the other members of The Folkstone Collection.

②

Values	
1E	$130
2E	$85
3E	$70
AE	$50

December 26th
#3003 • Original Price: $33
Issued: 1996 • Retired: 1997

③

Values	
1E	$110
2E	$67
3E	$55
AE	$47
Variation	
1E	$117
2E	$80
3E	$66
AE	$54

Nick On Ice (GRS)
#3001 • Original Price: $33
Issued: 1994 • Retired: 1997
Variation: original version

④

Values	
1E	$90
2E	$70
3E	$55
AE	$42
Variation	
1E	$110
2E	$82
3E	$66
AE	$47

Santa's Challenge (GRS)
#3002 • Original Price: $33
Issued: 1994 • Retired: 1997
Variation: original version

CARVERS CHOICE

SANTA & FRIENDS

	Date Purchased	Price Paid	Value Of My Collection
1.			
2.			
3.			
4.			
✏ PENCIL TOTALS			

①

Values	
1E	$92
2E	$74
3E	$55
AE	$45
Variation	
1E	$116
2E	$83
3E	$70
AE	$52

Santa's Flight Plan (GRS)
#3000 • Original Price: $33
Issued: 1994 • Retired: 1997
Variation: original version

②

Values	
1E	$88
2E	$62
3E	$57
AE	$44
Variation	
1E	$105
2E	$70
3E	$62
AE	$50

Santa's Hobby...
The Teddy Bear Maker
#3004 • Original Price: $35
Issued: 1996 • Retired: 1997
Variation: 1996 GCC Early Release

THE WEE FOLKSTONES

This set of diminutive angels and companions are designed to be placed in surprising, unexpected corners and crannies, just where one would expect to find a faerie! Guardian angels in training, these characters are sure to watch over every facet of life from the trials and tribulations of love to the stimulating effects of a good cup of coffee. With five introductions for Spring 1999, everyone can have a angel watching over their shoulder.

③

Values	
PR	$65
1E	$60
2E	$47
3E	$35
AE	$16

Angelina "Smidge" Angellove...
Angel Of True Love
#36100 • Original Price: $16
Issued: 1997 • To Be Retired: 12/31/99

SANTA & FRIENDS

	Date Purchased	Price Paid	Value Of My Collection
1.			
2.			

THE WEE FOLKSTONES

3.			
4.			

✎ PENCIL TOTALS

④

Values	
1E	$43
2E	$19
3E	$19
AE	$19

Bobby ... The Defender
#36505 • Original Price: $19
Issued: 1998 • Current

①

Values	
PR	$55
1E	$47
2E	$19
3E	$19
AE	$19

Caffeinata (Speedy) P. Faeriebean...
The Coffee Faerie
#36304 • Original Price: $19
Issued: 1998 • Current

②

Values	
1E	$40
2E	$18
3E	$18
AE	$18

Cerebella "Smarty" Faerienoggin
#36201 • Original Price: $18
Issued: 1998 • Current

③

Values	
1E	$38
2E	$16
3E	$16
AE	$16

Cicely & Juneau... Iced Tea Party
#36503 • Original Price: $16
Issued: 1998 • Current

④ New!

Values	
1E	$18
2E	$18
3E	$18
AE	$18

Confidentia "No-Tell" Faeriewhisper
#36105 • Original Price: $18
Issued: 1999 • Current

⑤

Values (U.S.)	
1E	$60
2E	$48
3E	$36
AE	$25

Dentinata Canadian Tooth Faerie
(Canadian Exclusive)
#BC361021 • Original Price: $24.99 (Can.)
Issued: 1997 • Current

THE WEE FOLKSTONES

	Date Purchased	Price Paid	Value Of My Collection
1.			
2.			
3.	1/30/99	Gift	
4.			
5.			
✎ PENCIL TOTALS			

FOLKSTONES

①

Values	
PR	$58
1E	$46
2E	$34
3E	$22
AE	$16

Dentinata "Faeriefloss" ...
The Tooth Faerie
#36102 • Original Price: $16
Issued: 1997 • To Be Retired: 12/31/99

②

Values	
PR	$55
1E	$48
2E	$35
3E	$27
AE	$18

"Electra" Angelbyte ...
Angel Of Computer Training
#36300 • Original Price: $18
Issued: 1997 • Current

③

Values	
1E	$48
2E	$30
3E	$25
AE	$18

Estudious "Cram" Faeriebaum ...
The Study Faerie
#36301 • Original Price: $18
Issued: 1997 • Current

④ **New!**

Values	
PR	$18
1E	$18
2E	$18
3E	$18
AE	$18

Felicity Angelbliss ...
The Bride's Angel
#36103 • Original Price: $18
Issued: 1999 • Current

THE WEE FOLKSTONES

	Date Purchased	Price Paid	Value Of My Collection
1.			
2.			
3.			
4.			
5.			
✎ PENCIL TOTALS			

⑤ **New!**

Values	
1E	$18
2E	$18
3E	$18
AE	$18

Fergus "Bogey" MacDivot
#36401 • Original Price: $18
Issued: 1999 • Current

FOLKSTONES

1

Values	
1E	$58
2E	$42
3E	$30
AE	$26

Fixit … Santa's Faerie
#3600 • Original Price: $18
Issued: 1996 • Retired: 1998

2

Values	
1E	$42
2E	$19
3E	$19
AE	$19

Flakey … Ice Sculptor
#36504 • Original Price: $19
Issued: 1998 • Current

3

Values	
PR	$43
1E	$35
2E	$26
3E	$22
AE	$18

Gabrielle "Gabby" Faeriejabber
#36003 • Original Price: $18
Issued: 1997 • To Be Retired: 12/31/99

4 New!

Values	
PR	$15
1E	$15
2E	$15
3E	$15
AE	$15

Grandma Faeriehugs
#36106 • Original Price: $15
Issued: 1999 • Current

5

Values	
1E	$33
2E	$24
3E	$19
AE	$14.50

Half Pipe … The Hot Dogger
#36502 • Original Price: $14.50
Issued: 1997 • Current

THE WEE FOLKSTONES

	Date Purchased	Price Paid	Value Of My Collection
1.			
2.			
3.			
4.			
5.			
PENCIL TOTALS			

①

Values	
PR	$59
1E	$50
2E	$34
3E	$26
AE	$18

Immaculata Faerieburg... The Cleaning Faerie
#36302 • Original Price: $18
Issued: 1997 • Current

②

Values	
PR	$46
1E	$35
2E	$19
3E	$19
AE	$19

Indulgenia Q. Bluit... Angel Of Denial
#36305 • Original Price: $19
Issued: 1998 • Current

③

Values	
1E	$50
2E	$32
3E	$26
AE	$20

Infiniti Faerielove... The Wedding Faerie
#36101 • Original Price: $16
Issued: 1997 • Retired: 1998

④

Value	
NE	$38

Katerina & Florence... Cold Comfort (GCC Exclusive)
#36402GCC • Original Price: $18.50
Issued: 1998 • Retired: 1998

THE WEE FOLKSTONES

	Date Purchased	Price Paid	Value Of My Collection
1.			
2.			
3.			
4.			
5.			
PENCIL TOTALS			

⑤

Values	
PR	$50
1E	$43
2E	$26
3E	$21
AE	$17

Kristabell Faeriefrost
#36002 • Original Price: $17
Issued: 1997 • Current
Variation: 1997 Premier Edition
"Astriel Faeriefrost"

①

Values	
PR	$47
1E	$40
2E	$18
3E	$18
AE	$18

Mangianata (Nosh) J. Faeriechild... The Cooking Faerie
#36303 • Original Price: $18
Issued: 1998 • Current

②

Values	
1E	$33
2E	$23
3E	$18
AE	$14.50

Pearl... The Knitter
#36501 • Original Price: $14.50
Issued: 1997 • Current

③

Values	
1E	$33
2E	$23
3E	$18
AE	$14.50

Pearl Too... The Knitter
#36501-1 • Original Price: $14.50
Issued: 1997 • Current

④

Values	
PR	$44
1E	$39
2E	$18
3E	$18
AE	$18

Remembrance Angelflyte... Time Flies
#36004 • Original Price: $18
Issued: 1998 • Current

⑤

Values	
1E	$40
2E	$24
3E	$19
AE	$14.50

Slurp And The Snowcone Stand
#36500 • Original Price: $14.50
Issued: 1997 • Current

THE WEE FOLKSTONES

	Date Purchased	Price Paid	Value Of My Collection
1.			
2.			
3.			
4.			
5.			
PENCIL TOTALS			

1

Values (U.S.)	
1E	$40
2E	$20
3E	$20
AE	$20

Stanley The Stick Handler
(Canadian Exclusive)
#BC36507 • Original Price: $20 (Can.)
Issued: 1998 • Current

2

Values	
1E	$77
2E	$54
3E	$38
AE	$20

T.H. Bean... The Bearmaker Elf
#36400 • Original Price: $20
Issued: 1997 • Current

3

New!

Values	
1E	$18
2E	$18
3E	$18
AE	$18

Tuxworth P. Cummerbund
#36104 • Original Price: $18
Issued: 1999 • Current

RIBBIT & CO.

This bunch of ambitious amphibians made a big splash with their 1998 debut as the newest sub-category of *The Wee Folkstones*. Whether fishing for flies, lying in wait for that mystical kiss or bringing holiday cheer, these critters are a reminder of all those fairy tales we heard as children. With three new pieces making their debut this season, this collection is sure to hop right into the hearts of collectors.

THE WEE FOLKSTONES

	Date Purchased	Price Paid	Value Of My Collection
1.			
2.			
3.			

RIBBIT & CO.

4.			
PENCIL TOTALS			

4

Values	
1E	$32
2E	$15
3E	$15
AE	$15

Bridges... Scuba Frog
#36751 • Original Price: $15
Issued: 1998 • To Be Retired: 12/31/99

FOLKSTONES

①

Values	
PR	$34
1E	$30
2E	$13
3E	$13
AE	$13

Charles Dunkleburger Prince Of Tales...Kiss Me Quick!
#36700 • Original Price: $13
Issued: 1998 • Current

②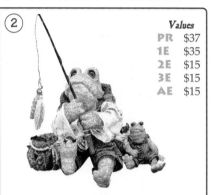

Values	
PR	$37
1E	$35
2E	$15
3E	$15
AE	$15

Frogmorton And Tad...Fly Fishing
#36701 • Original Price: $15
Issued: 1998 • Current

③

Values	
1E	$30
2E	$20
3E	$18
AE	$16

Jacques Grenouille... The Wine Taster
#36702 • Original Price: $14
Issued: 1998 • Retired: 1998

④ *New!*

Values	
1E	$14
2E	$14
3E	$14
AE	$14

Jeremiah "Jellybean" Pondhopper
#36704 • Original Price: $14
Issued: 1999 • Current

⑤ *New!*

Values	
1E	$14
2E	$14
3E	$14
AE	$14

Ms. Lilypond...Lesson #1
#36705 • Original Price: $14
Issued: 1999 • Current

RIBBIT & CO.

	Date Purchased	Price Paid	Value Of My Collection
1.			
2.			
3.			
4.			
5.			
PENCIL TOTALS			

①

Values
1E $30
2E $14
3E $14
AE $14

S.C. Ribbit ... Hoppy Christmas
#36750 • Original Price: $14
Issued: 1998 • Current

② New!

Values
1E $14
2E $14
3E $14
AE $14

TuTu C. Ribbit ... Frog Lake
#36703 • Original Price: $14
Issued: 1999 • Current

RIBBIT & CO.

	Date Purchased	Price Paid	Value Of My Collection
1.			
2.			
PENCIL TOTALS			

OTHER FOLKSTONE COLLECTIBLES

Those whimsical characters from all walks of Folkstone life, including *Carvers Choice*, *Ribbit & Co.* and *The Wee Folkstones*, are bringing their old-fashioned charm to a variety of pieces including a half dozen frames, a musical, 28 ornaments, a sconce, four votive holders and four water-globes. Four new pieces will join the collection this season.

Values	
1E	$36
2E	$21
3E	$21
AE	$21

Barnaby's Snow Sweep Service
Carvers Choice
#370301 • Original Price: $21
Issued: 1998 • Current

FOLKSTONES

Values	
1E	$34
2E	$21
3E	$21
AE	$21

Darby & Jasper ... Knitten' Kittens
#27451 • Original Price: $21
Issued: 1998 • Current

New!

Values	
1E	$24
2E	$24
3E	$24
AE	$24

Frogmorton & Tad ... Fly Fishing
Ribbit & Co.
#27402 • Original Price: $24
Issued: 1999 • Current

Values	
JAN	$41
FEB	$32
MAR	$30
APR-DEC	$29

Liddy Pearl ... They Grow Like Weeds (LE-1998)
#27450 • Original Price: $27
Issued: 1998 • Retired: 1998

FRAMES

	Date Purchased	Price Paid	Value Of My Collection
1.			
2.			
3.			
4.			
PENCIL TOTALS			

1

New!

Values	
1E	$21
2E	$21
3E	$21
AE	$21

Martha Bigheart ... Love Much
Carvers Choice
#370302 • Original Price: $21
Issued: 1999 • Current

2

Values	
1E	$35
2E	$21
3E	$21
AE	$21

Santa's Frame Shop
Carvers Choice
#370300 • Original Price: $21
Issued: 1998 • Current

3

New!

Values	
1E	$28
2E	$28
3E	$28
AE	$28

Cocoa M. Angelrich & Scoop
The Wee Folkstones
#271050 • Original Price: $28
Issued: 1999 • Current

4

Values	
1E	$25
2E	$12
3E	$12
AE	$12

Axel ... Thou Shalt Not Melt!
#26562 • Original Price: $12
Issued: 1997 • Current

FRAMES

	Date Purchased	Price Paid	Value Of My Collection
1.			
2.			

MUSICALS

3.			

ORNAMENTS

4.			
5.			
PENCIL TOTALS			

5

Values	
1E	$23
2E	$10
3E	$10
AE	$10

Barnaby ... Homeward Bound
Carvers Choice
#370201 • Original Price: $10
Issued: 1998 • Current

FOLKSTONES

①

Values	
1E	$20
2E	$12
3E	$12
AE	$12

Bjorn … With Nils & Sven
#25654 • Original Price: $12
Issued: 1998 • Current

②

Values	
1E	$23
2E	$10
3E	$10
AE	$10

Burt … Bundle Up
Carvers Choice
#370202 • Original Price: $10
Issued: 1998 • Current

③

Value	
NE	$17

Chilly With Wreath
#2564 • Original Price: $10
Issued: 1996 • Retired: 1998

④

Value	
NE	$28

Father Christmas
#2553 • Original Price: $10
Issued: 1995 • Retired: 1997

⑤

Values	
1E	$27
2E	$12
3E	$12
AE	$12

Ingrid … Be Warm
#25651 • Original Price: $12
Issued: 1997 • Current

ORNAMENTS

	Date Purchased	Price Paid	Value Of My Collection
1.			
2.			
3.			
4.			
5.			
PENCIL TOTALS			

1

Value
NE $36

Jacques … Starlight Skier (LE-1997)
#25950 • Original Price: $21
Issued: 1997 • Retired: 1997

2

Value
NE $29

Jean Claude & Jacque … The Skiers
#2561 • Original Price: $10
Issued: 1995 • Retired: 1997

3

Value
NE $37

Jingle Nick (QVC Exclusive)
#63711 • Original Price: N/A
Issued: 1996 • Retired: 1996

4

Value
NE $27

Jingles The Snowman With Wreath
#2562 • Original Price: $10
Issued: 1995 • Retired: 1997

ORNAMENTS

	Date Purchased	Price Paid	Value Of My Collection
1.			
2.			
3.			
4.			
5.			
PENCIL TOTALS			

5

Value
NE $32

Joy (GCC Exclusive)
#25653GCC • Original Price: $10
Issued: 1997 • Retired: 1997

①

Values	
1E	$20
2E	$12
3E	$12
AE	$12

Lars…Ski, Ski, Ski
#25653 • Original Price: $12
Issued: 1998 • Current

②

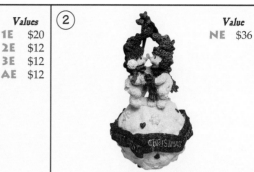

Value	
NE	$36

Mistletoe & Holly –
First Christmas "1997" (LE-1997)
#25900 • Original Price: $14
Issued: 1997 • Retired: 1997

③

Values	
1E	$32
2E	$21
3E	$21
AE	$21

Nanuk…Winter Wonderland
#25956 • Original Price: $21
Issued: 1998 • Current

④

Value	
NE	$27

Nicholai With Tree
#2550 • Original Price: $10
Issued: 1995 • Retired: 1997

⑤

Value	
NE	$27

Nicholas The Giftgiver
#2551 • Original Price: $10
Issued: 1995 • Retired: 1997

FOLKSTONES

ORNAMENTS

	Date Purchased	Price Paid	Value Of My Collection
1.			
2.			
3.			
4.			
5.			
✏ PENCIL TOTALS			

(1)

Value	
NE	$27

Olaf ... Let It Snow
#2560 • Original Price: $10
Issued: 1995 • Retired: 1997

(2)

Values	
1E	$26
2E	$12
3E	$12
AE	$12

Olaf ... Let It Snow
#25650 • Original Price: $12
Issued: 1997 • Current

(3)

Values	
1E	$32
2E	$12
3E	$12
AE	$12

Olivia ... Wishing You "Peace"
The Wee Folkstones
#25800 • Original Price: $12
Issued: 1998 • Current

(4)

Values	
1E	$25
2E	$12
3E	$12
AE	$12

Robin ... Peace On Earth
#25655 • Original Price: $12
Issued: 1998 • Current

ORNAMENTS

	Date Purchased	Price Paid	Value Of My Collection
1.			
2.			
3.			
4.			
5.			
PENCIL TOTALS			

(5)

Values	
1E	$23
2E	$10
3E	$10
AE	$10

Santa ... And The Final Inspection
Carvers Choice
#370203 • Original Price: $10
Issued: 1998 • Current

FOLKSTONES

**① **

Values	
1E	$23
2E	$10
3E	$10
AE	$10

Santa... In The Nick Of Time
Carvers Choice
#370200 • Original Price: $10
Issued: 1998 • Current

②

Values	
1E	$23
2E	$10
3E	$10
AE	$10

Santa... Quick As A Flash
Carvers Choice
#370204 • Original Price: $10
Issued: 1998 • Current

③

Value	
NE	$26

Sliknick In The Chimney
#2552 • Original Price: $10
Issued: 1995 • Retired: 1997

④

Value	
NE	$42

Starry Starry Night (QVC Exclusive)
#63714 • Original Price: N/A
Issued: 1996 • Retired: 1996

⑤

Value	
NE	$16

Willie With Broom
#2565 • Original Price: $10
Issued: 1996 • Retired: 1998

ORNAMENTS

	Date Purchased	Price Paid	Value Of My Collection
1.			
2.			
3.			
4.			
5.			
PENCIL TOTALS			

141

1

	Value
NE	$16

Windy With Tree
#2563 • Original Price: $10
Issued: 1996 • Retired: 1998

2

	Values
1E	$33
2E	$17
3E	$17
AE	$17

"Think" Library Book
#65427 • Original Price: $17
Issued: 1998 • Current

3

New!

	Values
1E	$27
2E	$27
3E	$27
AE	$27

Audubon P. Pussywillow ...
The Birdwatcher
#27803 • Original Price: $27
Issued: 1999 • Current

4

	Values
1E	$40
2E	$27
3E	$27
AE	$27

Darby & Jasper ... Knitten' Kittens
#27802 • Original Price: $27
Issued: 1998 • Current

ORNAMENTS

	Date Purchased	Price Paid	Value Of My Collection
1.			

SCONCES

2.			

VOTIVE HOLDERS

3.			
4.			
5.			

PENCIL TOTALS

5

	Values
1E	$42
2E	$27
3E	$27
AE	$27

Ingrid & Olaf ... Be Warm
#27801 • Original Price: $27
Issued: 1998 • Current

①

Values	
1E	$48
2E	$40
3E	$27
AE	$27

Yukon & Kodiak...
Nome Sweet Home
#27800 • Original Price: $27
Issued: 1997 • Current

②

Values	
1E	$84
2E	$55
3E	$42
AE	$37

Jean Claude & Jacque... The Skiers
#2710 • Original Price: $37
Issued: 1996 • Current

③

Value	
NE	$70

Liddy Pearl... How Does Your
Garden Grow (LE-1998)
#270602 • Original Price: $53
Issued: 1998 • Retired: 1998

④

Value	
NE	$75

Santa's Flight Plan
#2703 • Original Price: $36
Issued: 1995 • Retired: 1996

⑤

Values	
1E	$50
2E	$39
3E	$39
AE	$39

Yukon, Kodiak & Nanuk...
Nome Sweet Home
#271001 • Original Price: $39
Issued: 1997 • Current

VOTIVE HOLDERS

	Date Purchased	Price Paid	Value Of My Collection
1.			

WATERGLOBES

2.			
3.			
4.			
5.			
✎ PENCIL TOTALS			

FOLKWEAR PINS

The most stylish collectors know that Folkwear pins are topping the collectibles fashion charts. While this season's introduction of nine new pins brings the collection's total to 66, many have been retired.

1

Alice & Emily
Issued: 1996 • Retired
#2666 • *Value: $7*

2

Angelina...
Key To My Heart
Issued: 1998 • Current
#26319 • *Value: $4*

3

Ariel... The Guardian
Issued: 1996 • Retired
#2671 • *Value: $6*

4

Ashley The Angel
Issued: 1996 • Current
#26303 • *Value: $4*

5 New!

Auntie Cocoa...
Life Is Short
Issued: 1999 • Current
#26421 • *Value: $4*

6

Axel... Let It Snow
Issued: 1998 • Current
#26317 • *Value: $4*

FOLKWEAR PINS

	Price Paid	Value Of My Collection
1.		
2.		
3.		
4.		
5.		
6.		
7.		
8.		
9.		
10.		
11.		
12.		
13.		
14.		
15.		
16.		
17.		
18.		
PENCIL TOTALS		

7

Baby Amelia's Carrot Juice
Issued: 1997 • Retired
#26404 • *Value: $8*

8

Barnaby... Homeward Bound
Carvers Choice
Issued: 1998 • Current
#370501 • *Value: $4*

9

Bearly Santa
Issued: 1997 • Retired
#26311 • *Value: $7*

10

Beatrice's Wreath
Issued: 1995 • Retired
#2638 • *Value: $7*

11

Bessie With Sun Flowers
Issued: 1996 • Current
#2664 • *Value: $4*

12

Betty Biscuit
Issued: 1997 • Retired
#26403 • *Value: $8*

13

Daphne In Straw Hat
Issued: 1996 • Retired
#2668 • *Value: $8*

14

Egads... The Skier
Issued: 1997 • Retired
#26308 • *Value: $8*

15

Eloise In The Cabbage Patch
Issued: 1996 • Current
#2661 • *Value: $4*

16

Eloise... Tea Toter
Issued: 1997 • Retired
#26402 • *Value: $8*

17

Esmeralda The Witch
Issued: 1996 • Retired
#26304 • *Value: $10*

18

Fenton J. Padworthy...
The Formal Frog
Issued: 1998 • Retired
#26412 • *Value: $8*

① New!
Flora...Hoppy Spring
Issued: 1999 • Current
#26418 • *Value:* $4

②
Florence Wings It
Issued: 1995 • Retired
#2625 • *Value:* $8

③
Florina's Wreath
Issued: 1997 • Retired
#26400 • *Value:* $8

④
"Flossie"...Keep Smiling
Issued: 1998 • Retired
#26411 • *Value:* $6

⑤ New!
Frogmorton...
Fish, Lie, Fish
Issued: 1999 • Current
#26415 • *Value:* $4

⑥
Frogmorton...
Pad Sweet Pad
Issued: 1998 • Retired
#26414 • *Value:* $6

⑦
Frosty Kristabell
Issued: 1997 • Retired
#26309 • *Value:* $7

⑧ New!
Harriet...Farm Fresh
Issued: 1999 • Current
#26423 • *Value:* $4

⑨
Helga...Be Warm
Issued: 1998 • Current
#26318 • *Value:* $4

⑩ New!
Immaculata...Scrub-A-Dub!
Issued: 1999 • Current
#26422 • *Value:* $4

⑪ New!
Jasper...Knittin' Kitten
Issued: 1999 • Current
#26417 • *Value:* $4

⑫
Jean Claude The Skier
Issued: 1995 • Retired
#2651 • *Value:* $8

⑬
Jingles With Wreath
Issued: 1996 • Retired
#26302 • *Value:* $8

⑭
Lars...Bells Are Ringing
Issued: 1997 • Retired
#26306 • *Value:* $7

⑮
Madge...
Beautician/Magician
Issued: 1998 • Retired
#26406 • *Value:* $7

⑯
McDivot...Golf, Lie, Golf
Issued: 1998 • Retired
#26409 • *Value:* $6

⑰
Melvin...The Jingle Moose
Issued: 1997 • Retired
#26307 • *Value:* $9

⑱
Minerva With Daffodils
Issued: 1996 • Current
#2658 • *Value:* $4

⑲
Minerva's Flight
Issued: 1995 • Retired
#2647 • *Value:* $10

⑳ New!
Ms. McFrazzle...Care Giver
Issued: 1999 • Current
#26420 • *Value:* $4

FOLKWEAR PINS

	Price Paid	Value Of My Collection
1.		
2.		
3.		
4.		
5.		
6.		
7.		
8.		
9.		
10.		
11.		
12.		
13.		
14.		
15.		
16.		
17.		
18.		
19.		
20.		
PENCIL TOTALS		

FOLKSTONES

#	Name	Issued	Status	Item #	Value
1	Ms. Patience… Teach, Learn	Issued: 1998	Current	#26405	Value: $4
2	Ms. Patience… The Teacher	Issued: 1997	Retired	#26401	Value: $8
3	Ms. Prudence… Teach, Learn (New!)	Issued: 1999	Current	#26416	Value: $4
4	Nana & Aubergine & Peapod	Issued: 1998	Current	#26407	Value: $4
5	Na-Nick Of The North	Issued: 1995	Current	#2650	Value: $4
6	Nicholai…With Dove	Issued: 1995	Retired	#2648	Value: $10
7	Nicholai With Tree	Issued: 1996	Retired	#26300	Value: $10
8	Nicholas…With Tree	Issued: 1995	Retired	#2649	Value: $10
9	Nome Sweet Home	Issued: 1997	Retired	#26310	Value: $7
10	"Nosh"… What's Cooking?!?!	Issued: 1998	Retired	#26408	Value: $6
11	Oceania	Issued: 1996	Retired	#2674	Value: $8
12	Olaf…I Luuv Snow	Issued: 1998	Current	#26321	Value: $4
13	Olaf… The Flakey Snowman	Issued: 1997	Retired	#26305	Value: $8
14	Peacenik Santa	Issued: 1997	Retired	#26314	Value: $8
15	Purrscilla & Friends (New!)	Issued: 1999	Current	#26419	Value: $4
16	Ralph Angel Pooch	Issued: 1996	Retired	#2669	Value: $7
17	Sabrina… Bippity Boppity Boo!	Issued: 1998	Current	#26315	Value: $4
18	Santa… And The Final Inspection *Carvers Choice*	Issued: 1998	Current	#370503	Value: $4
19	Santa… In The Nick Of Time *Carvers Choice*	Issued: 1998	Current	#370500	Value: $4
20	Santa… Quick As A Flash *Carvers Choice*	Issued: 1998	Current	#370504	Value: $4

FOLKWEAR PINS

	Price Paid	Value Of My Collection
1.		
2.		
3.		
4.		
5.		
6.		
7.		
8.		
9.		
10.		
11.		
12.		
13.		
14.		
15.		
16.		
17.		
18.		
19.		
20.		
PENCIL TOTALS		

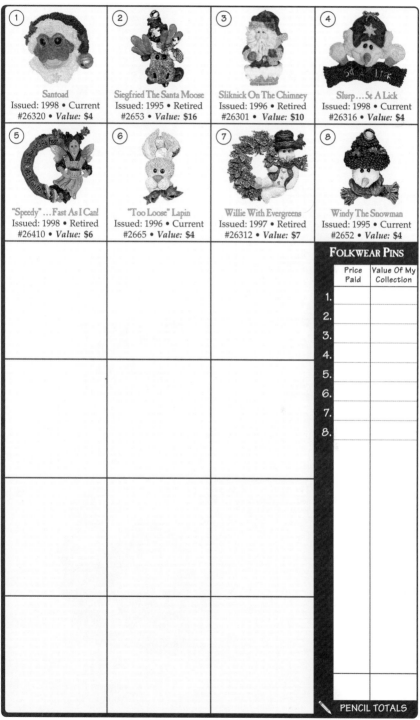

① Santoad
Issued: 1998 • Current
#26320 • *Value:* **$4**

② Siegfried The Santa Moose
Issued: 1995 • Retired
#2653 • *Value:* **$16**

③ Sliknick On The Chimney
Issued: 1996 • Retired
#26301 • *Value:* **$10**

④ Slurp...5¢ A Lick
Issued: 1998 • Current
#26316 • *Value:* **$4**

⑤ "Speedy"...Fast As I Can!
Issued: 1998 • Retired
#26410 • *Value:* **$6**

⑥ "Too Loose" Lapin
Issued: 1996 • Current
#2665 • *Value:* **$4**

⑦ Willie With Evergreens
Issued: 1997 • Retired
#26312 • *Value:* **$7**

⑧ Windy The Snowman
Issued: 1995 • Current
#2652 • *Value:* **$4**

FOLKWEAR PINS

	Price Paid	Value Of My Collection
1.		
2.		
3.		
4.		
5.		
6.		
7.		
8.		

✎ PENCIL TOTALS

FOLKSTONES

GENERAL FIGURINES

With this season's release of six new pieces, The Dollstone Collection grows to 49 figurines. While one can only wish for the return of these simpler times, with themes ranging from a ballerina preparing for her solo to friends combing the beach for treasures, The Dollstone Collection provides a touching reminder of those times gone by.

① New!

Values	
1E	$18
2E	$18
3E	$18
AE	$18

Alyssa With Caroline...
A Stitch In Time

#3539 • Original Price: $18
Issued: 1999 • Current

---

②

Values	
PR	$150
JAN	$115
FEB	$90
MAR	$82
APR-DEC	$68

The Amazing Bailey...
"Magic Show At 4" (LE-1997)

#3518 • Original Price: $58
Issued: 1997 • Retired: 1997

---

③

Values	
PR	$72
1E	$55
2E	$40
3E	$34
AE	$30

Amy And Edmund...
Momma's Clothes

#3529 • Original Price: $30
Issued: 1998 • Current

GENERAL FIGURINES

	Date Purchased	Price Paid	Value Of My Collection
1.			
2.			
3.			
4.			
✎ PENCIL TOTALS			

---

④

Values	
1E	$80
2E	$55
3E	$39
AE	$25

Anne... The Masterpiece

#3599 • Original Price: $25
Issued: 1996 • Current

①

Values	
PR	$82
1E	$72
2E	$44
3E	$36
AE	$20.50

Ashley With Chrissie… Dress Up
#3506 • Original Price: $20.50
Issued: 1996 • To Be Retired: 12/31/99

②

Values	
PR	$60
1E	$52
2E	$40
3E	$30
AE	$20

Austin & Allen… The Fire Chief
#3534 • Original Price: $20
Issued: 1998 • Current

③

Values	
PR	$72
1E	$65
2E	$43
3E	$34
AE	$29

Benjamin With Matthew… The Speed Trap
#3524 • Original Price: $29
Issued: 1997 • Current

④

Values (U.S.)	
1E	$85
2E	$67
3E	$49
AE	$35

Betsey And Edmund With Union Jack (Canadian Exclusive)
#BC35031 • Original Price: $29.99 (Can.)
Issued: 1996 • Current

⑤

Values	
PR	$145
1E	$94
2E	$56
3E	$42
AE	$20

Betsey With Edmund… The Patriots
#3503 • Original Price: $20
Issued: 1996 • Current

DOLLSTONES

GENERAL FIGURINES

	Date Purchased	Price Paid	Value Of My Collection
1.			
2.			
3.			
4.			
5.			
PENCIL TOTALS			

①

Values	
PR	$69
1E	$60
2E	$43
3E	$36
AE	$20

Caitlin With Emma & Edmund... Diapering Baby

#3525 • Original Price: $20
Issued: 1997 • To Be Retired: 12/31/99

②

Values	
PR	$76
1E	$65
2E	$43
3E	$36
AE	$19

Candice With Matthew... Gathering Apples

#3514 • Original Price: $19
Issued: 1996 • To Be Retired: 12/31/99

③

Values	
1E	$80
2E	$52
3E	$48
AE	$35

Courtney With Phoebe... Over The River And Thru The Woods

#3512 • Original Price: $25
Issued: 1996 • Retired: 1997

④

Values	
1E	$105
2E	$85
3E	$72
AE	$48

Courtney With Phoebe... Over The River And Thru The Woods (GCC Exclusive)

#3512-01 • Original Price: $27.50
Issued: 1996 • Retired: 1996

GENERAL FIGURINES

	Date Purchased	Price Paid	Value Of My Collection
1.	Ma -		
2.			
3.			
4.			
5.			
 PENCIL TOTALS			

⑤

Value	
NE	$130

Elizabeth And Gary (figurine and porcelain doll set, QVC Exclusive, LE-25,000)

N/A • Original Price: $116
Issued: 1998 • Retired: 1998

① **Values**

PR	$110
1E	$84
2E	$56
3E	$46
AE	$30

Emily With Kathleen & Otis...
The Future
#3508 • Original Price: $30
Issued: 1996 • Current

② New!

Values

1E	$20
2E	$20
3E	$20
AE	$20

Heather With Lauren...
Bunny Helpers
#3538 • Original Price: $20
Issued: 1999 • Current

③

Values

PR	$60
1E	$52
2E	$38
3E	$26
AE	$20

Jamie And Thomasina...
The Last One
#3530 • Original Price: $20
Issued: 1998 • Current

④

Values

PR	$70
1E	$62
2E	$45
3E	$33
AE	$20

Jean With Elliot & Debbie...
The Bakers
#3510 • Original Price: $20
Issued: 1996 • Current

⑤

Value

NE	$95

Jean With Elliot & Debbie...
The Bakers (Kirlin's Exclusive)
#3510-01 • Original Price: $20
Issued: 1996 • Retired: 1996

DOLLSTONES

GENERAL FIGURINES

	Date Purchased	Price Paid	Value Of My Collection
1.			
2.			
3.			
4.			
5.			
PENCIL TOTALS			

1

Values	
PR	$210
1E	$96
2E	$63
3E	$48
AE	$35

Jennifer With Priscilla... The Doll In The Attic

#3500 • Original Price: $20.50
Issued: 1996 • Retired: 1997

2

Values	
JAN	$90
FEB	$64
MAR	$47
APR-DEC	$43

Jessica And Timmy... Animal Hospital (LE-1998)

#3532 • Original Price: $40
Issued: 1998 • Retired: 1998

3

Values	
PR	$68
1E	$55
2E	$37
3E	$29
AE	$20

Julia With Emmy Lou & Daphne... Garden Friends

#3520 • Original Price: $20
Issued: 1997 • Current

4

Values	
1E	$62
2E	$51
3E	$36
AE	$28

Karen With Wilson & Eloise... Mother's Present

#3515-01 • Original Price: $20
Issued: 1997 • Retired: 1998

GENERAL FIGURINES

	Date Purchased	Price Paid	Value Of My Collection
1.			
2.			
3.			
4.	MA~ 7E/4699 10-23-99	20.00	
5.			
✏ PENCIL TOTALS			

5

Values	
1E	$75
2E	$56
3E	$48
AE	$33

Karen With Wilson & Eloise... Mother's Present (GCC Exclusive)

#3515GCC • Original Price: $26
Issued: 1996 • Retired: 1996

(1)

Values	
PR	$168
1E	$87
2E	$65
3E	$45
AE	$20

Katherine With Edmund & Amanda ... Kind Hearts
#3505 • Original Price: $20
Issued: 1996 • Current

(2) New!

Values	
JAN	$36
FEB	$36
MAR	$36
APR-DEC	$36

Kelly And Company ... The Bear Collector (LE-1999)
#3542 • Original Price: $36
Issued: 1999 • To Be Retired: 1999

(3)

Values	
1E	$65
2E	$50
3E	$38
AE	$26
Variation	
NE	$87

Kristi With Nicole ... Skater's Waltz
#3516 • Original Price: $26
Issued: 1996 • Current
Variation: 1996 GCC Early Release

(4)

Values	
PR	$72
1E	$55
2E	$38
3E	$32
AE	$23

Laura With Jane ... First Day Of School
#3522 • Original Price: $23
Issued: 1997 • Current

(5)

Values	
PR	$62
1E	$44
2E	$31
3E	$23
AE	$18

Lindsey With Louise ... The Recital
#3535 • Original Price: $18
Issued: 1998 • Current

DOLLSTONES

GENERAL FIGURINES

	Date Purchased	Price Paid	Value Of My Collection
1.	Ma ~		
2.			
3.	Ma ~		
4.			
5.	X		23
✏ PENCIL TOTALS			

① New!

Values	
1E	$18
2E	$18
3E	$18
AE	$18

Lucinda And Dawn... By The Sea
#3536 • Original Price: $18
Issued: 1999 • Current

②

Values	
PR	$160
1E	$82
2E	$59
3E	$42
AE	$27

Mallory With Patsy & J.B. Bean... Trick Or Treat
#3517 • Original Price: $27
Issued: 1996 • Current

③

Value	
NE	$39

Mary And Paul... The Prayer (LE-1998)
#3531-01 • Original Price: $16
Issued: 1998 • Retired: 1998

④

Values	
PR	$335
1E	$82
2E	$53
3E	$45
AE	$20

Megan With Elliot And Annie... Christmas Carol
#3504 • Original Price: $20
Issued: 1996 • Current

GENERAL FIGURINES

	Date Purchased	Price Paid	Value Of My Collection
1.			
2.			
3.			
4.	Ma —		45
5.			
PENCIL TOTALS			

⑤ New!

Values	
1E	$18
2E	$18
3E	$18
AE	$18

Melissa With Katie... The Ballet
#3537 • Original Price: $18
Issued: 1999 • Current

(1) New!

Values	
1E	$18
2E	$18
3E	$18
AE	$18

Meredith With Jacqueline...
Daisy Chain
#3541 • Original Price: $18
Issued: 1999 • Current

(2)

Values	
PR	$73
1E	$63
2E	$45
3E	$32
AE	$18

Michelle With Daisy...
Reading Is Fun
#3511 • Original Price: $18
Issued: 1996 • Current

(3)

Values	
1E	$72
2E	$53
3E	$43
AE	$23

Natalie With Joy...Sunday School
#3519 • Original Price: $23
Issued: 1997 • To Be Retired: 12/31/99

(4)

Values	
PR	$205
1E	$82
2E	$62
3E	$48
AE	$14

Patricia With Molly...
Attic Treasures
#3501 • Original Price: $14
Issued: 1996 • To Be Retired: 12/31/99

(5)

Values	
PR	$100
1E	$67
2E	$45
3E	$32
AE	$23

Rachael, Barbara & Matthew...
Sabbath Lights
#3526 • Original Price: $23
Issued: 1998 • To Be Retired: 12/31/99

GENERAL FIGURINES

	Date Purchased	Price Paid	Value Of My Collection
1.			
2.			
3.			
4.			
5.			
PENCIL TOTALS			

DOLLSTONES

155

①

Values	
PR	$75
1E	$62
2E	$46
3E	$38
AE	$21

Rebecca With Elliot ... Birthday
#3509 • Original Price: $21
Issued: 1996 • Current

②

Values	
PR	$100
1E	$65
2E	$52
3E	$46
AE	$39

Sandra Claus ... Christmas Morning
#3528-1 • Original Price: $39
Issued: 1998 • Current

③

Values	
PR	$162
1E	$120
2E	$98
3E	$85
AE	$72

Sarah & Heather With Elliot, Dolly & Amelia ... Tea For Four (LE-1996)
#3507 • Original Price: $47
Issued: 1996 • Retired: 1996

④

Values	
PR	$80
1E	$72
2E	$54
3E	$44
AE	$34

Shannon & Wilson ... Wait'n For Grandma
#3533 • Original Price: $34
Issued: 1998 • Current

General Figurines

	Date Purchased	Price Paid	Value Of My Collection
1.			
2.			
3.			
4.			
✏ PENCIL TOTALS			

①

Values	
PR	$55
1E	$39
2E	$34
3E	$26
AE	$15

Shelby ... Asleep In Teddy's Arms
#3527 • Original Price: $15
Issued: 1998 • Current

② New!

Values	
1E	$26
2E	$26
3E	$26
AE	$26

Stephanie With Jim ... School Days
#3540 • Original Price: $26
Issued: 1999 • Current

③

Values	
PR	$48
1E	$35
2E	$30
3E	$25
AE	$14

Teresa And John ... The Prayer
#3531 • Original Price: $14
Issued: 1998 • Current

④

Values	
PR	$152
1E	$86
2E	$70
3E	$55
AE	$20

**Victoria With Samantha ...
Victorian Ladies**
#3502 • Original Price: $20
Issued: 1996 • To Be Retired: 12/31/99

DOLLSTONES

GENERAL FIGURINES

	Date Purchased	Price Paid	Value Of My Collection
1.			
2.			
3.			
4.	✗		55
PENCIL TOTALS			

①

Values	
PR	$85
1E	$70
2E	$53
3E	$46
AE	$35

Wendy With Bronte, Keats, Tennyson & Poe...Wash Day
#3521 • Original Price: $23
Issued: 1997 • Retired: 1998

②

Values	
1E	$53
2E	$44
3E	$30
AE	$20

Whitney With Wilson...Tea Party
#3523 • Original Price: $20
Issued: 1997 • Current

OTHER DOLLSTONE COLLECTIBLES

The Dollstone Collection brings a glimpse of the simpler times to many facets of the chaos of everyday life. Featuring frames, musicals, ornaments, porcelain dolls, votive holders and waterglobes, this category is growing by the season, with 10 new releases this Spring.

③ *New!*

Values	
1E	$24
2E	$24
3E	$24
AE	$24

Lindsey With Louise...The Recital
#27551 • Original Price: $24
Issued: 1999 • Current

GENERAL FIGURINES

	Date Purchased	Price Paid	Value Of My Collection
1.			
2.	X		30

FRAMES

3.			
4.			
✏ PENCIL TOTALS			

④

Values	
1E	$42
2E	$25
3E	$25
AE	$25

Tiffany..."Forever"
#27550 • Original Price: $25
Issued: 1998 • Current

①

Values	
1E	$68
2E	$37
3E	$37
AE	$37

**Emily With Kathleen & Otis...
The Future**
#272052 • Original Price: $37
Issued: 1998 • Current

② *New!*

Values	
1E	$37
2E	$37
3E	$37
AE	$37

Grace & Faith... I Have A Dream
#272054 • Original Price: $37
Issued: 1999 • Current

③

Values	
PR	$77
1E	$74
2E	$60
3E	$44
AE	$37

Whitney With Wilson... Tea Party
#272001 • Original Price: $37
Issued: 1997 • Current

④

Value	
NE	$10

**Candice With Matthew...
Gathering Apples**
#25851 • Original Price: $10
Issued: 1998 • Current

⑤

Value	
NE	$10

Jean With Elliot... The Bakers
#25852 • Original Price: $10
Issued: 1998 • Current

MUSICALS

	Date Purchased	Price Paid	Value Of My Collection
1.			
2.			
3.	Ma~		44

ORNAMENTS

4.			
5.			
PENCIL TOTALS			

DOLLSTONES

①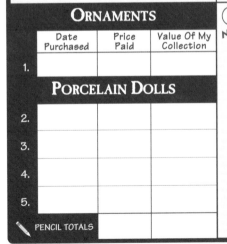

Value
NE $10

Megan With Elliot... Christmas Carol
#25850 • Original Price: $10
Issued: 1998 • Current

②
Value
NE $120

Betsy... Sail Away (LE-12,000)
#4904 • Original Price: $69
Issued: 1998 • Retired: 1998

③

Value
NE $100

Brittany... Life's Journey (LE-24,000)
#4906 • Original Price: $74
Issued: 1998 • Retired: 1998

④
Value
NE $128

Emily... The Future (LE-12,000)
#4902 • Original Price: $82
Issued: 1998 • Retired: 1998

ORNAMENTS

	Date Purchased	Price Paid	Value Of My Collection
1.			

PORCELAIN DOLLS

2.			
3.			
4.			
5.			
PENCIL TOTALS			

⑤ New!

Value
NE $69

Erin... Lemonade For Two (LE-12,000)
#4915 • Original Price: $69
Issued: 1999 • To Be Retired: 1999

①

Value
NE $100

Jamie...The Last One (LE-12,000)
#4908 • Original Price: $69
Issued: 1998 • Retired: 1998

②

Value
NE $150

Jamie...The Last One
(LE-2,000, QVC Exclusive)
N/A • Original Price: $66
Issued: 1998 • Retired: 1998

③ New!

Value
NE $72

Julia...Garden Friends (LE-18,000)
#4912 • Original Price: $72
Issued: 1999 • To Be Retired: 1999

④

Value
NE $165

Karen...Country Doll (LE-9,600)
#4900 • Original Price: $63
Issued: 1997 • Retired: 1997

⑤ New!

Value
NE $69

Katherine...Kind Hearts (LE-12,000)
#4910 • Original Price: $69
Issued: 1999 • To Be Retired: 1999

DOLLSTONES

PORCELAIN DOLLS

	Date Purchased	Price Paid	Value Of My Collection
1.			
2.			
3.			
4.			
5.			
✏ PENCIL TOTALS			

1 New!

Value
NE $67

Kelly The Bear Collector
(LE-12,000, QVC Exclusive)
N/A • Original Price: $67
Issued: 1999 • To Be Retired: 1999

2

Value
NE $100

Lara...Moscow At Midnight
(LE-12,000)
#4907 • Original Price: $71
Issued: 1998 • Retired: 1998

3

Value
NE $115

Laura...First Day Of School
(LE-12,000)
#4903 • Original Price: $69
Issued: 1998 • Retired: 1998

4 New!

Value
NE $69

Melissa...The Ballet (LE-12,000)
#4914 • Original Price: $69
Issued: 1999 • To Be Retired: 1999

PORCELAIN DOLLS

	Date Purchased	Price Paid	Value Of My Collection
1.			
2.			
3.			
4.			
5.			
✏ PENCIL TOTALS			

5

Value
NE $100

Ms. Ashley...The Teacher
(LE-12,000)
#4905 • Original Price: $69
Issued: 1998 • Retired: 1998

①

	Value
NE	$175

Victoria ... City Doll (LE-9,600)
#4901 • Original Price: $63
Issued: 1997 • Retired: 1997

② New!

	Value
NE	$72

Wendy ... Wash Day (LE-12,000)
#4909 • Original Price: $72
Issued: 1999 • To Be Retired: 1999

③ New!

	Values
1E	$27
2E	$27
3E	$27
AE	$27

Lucinda And Dawn ... By The Sea
#27951 • Original Price: $27
Issued: 1999 • Current

④

	Values
1E	$45
2E	$20
3E	$20
AE	$20

Teresa & John ... The Prayer
#27900 • Original Price: $20
Issued: 1998 • Current

⑤

	Values
1E	$54
2E	$45
3E	$36
AE	$26

**Whitney With Wilson ...
Tea And Candlelight**
#27950 • Original Price: $26
Issued: 1997 • To Be Retired: 12/31/99

PORCELAIN DOLLS

	Date Purchased	Price Paid	Value Of My Collection
1.			
2.			

VOTIVE HOLDERS

3.			
4.			
5.			
✎ PENCIL TOTALS			

DOLLSTONES

163

(1)

Values	
1E	$90
2E	$72
3E	$54
AE	$44

Megan With Elliot... Christmas Carol
(limited to one year of production)
#2720 • Original Price: $39
Issued: 1996 • Retired: 1997

(2) New!

Values	
1E	$38
2E	$38
3E	$38
AE	$38

Ryan & Diane... Love Is Forever
#272053 • Original Price: $38
Issued: 1999 • Current

(3) New!

Values	
1E	$50
2E	$50
3E	$50
AE	$50

Gardening Friends
♪ *Where Have All The Flowers Gone?*
#2776SF • Original Price: $50
Issued: 1999 • Current

(4) New!

Values	
1E	$45
2E	$45
3E	$45
AE	$45

Goin' To Grandma's
♪ *It's A Long Way To Tipperary*
#2775SF • Original Price: $45
Issued: 1999 • Current

WATERGLOBES

	Date Purchased	Price Paid	Value Of My Collection
1.			
2.			

SAN FRANCISCO MUSIC BOXES

3.			
4.			
5.			
✏ PENCIL TOTALS			

(5)

Values	
1E	$68
2E	$45
3E	$45
AE	$45

Wendy With Bronte, Keats, Tennyson And Poe... Wash Day
♪ *You Are So Beautiful*
#2711SF • Original Price: $45
Issued: 1998 • Current

THE SHOE BOX BEARS

The other Shoe Box Bears in the "joint" welcomed three new members to the family this season, with a good mind to keep an eye on things. Sgt. Bookum O'Reilly has arrived to keep order among the relatives while Ellie and Momma will do their best to keep those pesty eggs in line. While 1998 brought the retirement of the last bears to be less than fully attired, the three new pieces continue the trend of sporting highly detailed outfits.

(1)

Values	
PR	$55
1E	$44
2E	$29
3E	$25
AE	$22

Augustus "Gus" Grizberg
#3200 • Original Price: $19
Issued: 1996 • Retired: 1998

(2)

Values	
1E	$60
2E	$33
3E	$26
AE	$10

Elias "The Elf" Grizberg
#3206 • Original Price: $10
Issued: 1997 • Current

(3) New!

Values	
1E	$11
2E	$11
3E	$11
AE	$11

Ellie Grizberg ... Egg Hunter
#3212 • Original Price: $11
Issued: 1999 • Current

(4)

Values	
1E	$46
2E	$32
3E	$23
AE	$17

Filbert Q. Foghorn ...
The Commodore
#3208 • Original Price: $17
Issued: 1998 • Current

THE SHOE BOX BEARS

	Date Purchased	Price Paid	Value Of My Collection
1.			
2.			
3.			
4.			
✎ PENCIL TOTALS			

SHOE BOX BEARS

1

Values	
PR	$54
1E	$47
2E	$36
3E	$28
AE	$19

Gertrude "Gertie" Grizberg
#3201 • Original Price: $15
Issued: 1996 • Retired: 1998

2

Value	
NE	$60

Gladys (NALED Exclusive)
#3201-01 • Original Price: $15
Issued: 1996 • Retired: 1996

3

Values	
1E	$49
2E	$35
3E	$27
AE	$16

Maisey "The Goil" Grizberg
#3203 • Original Price: $10
Issued: 1997 • Retired: 1998

4

Values	
1E	$48
2E	$32
3E	$24
AE	$17

Miles "Gobble" Grizberg
#3209 • Original Price: $17
Issued: 1998 • Current

THE SHOE BOX BEARS

	Date Purchased	Price Paid	Value Of My Collection
1.			
2.			
3.			
4.			
5.			
PENCIL TOTALS			

5

New!

Values	
1E	$14
2E	$14
3E	$14
AE	$14

Momma Grizberg ... Egg Decorator
#3211 • Original Price: $14
Issued: 1999 • Current

①

Values	
1E	$46
2E	$35
3E	$26
AE	$20

Nicholas "Uncle Nick" Grizberg
#3205 • Original Price: $20
Issued: 1997 • Current

② New!

Values	
1E	$15
2E	$15
3E	$15
AE	$15

**Sgt. Bookum O'Reilly ...
To Protect & Serve**
#3214 • Original Price: $15
Issued: 1999 • Current

③

Values	
PR	$48
1E	$44
2E	$26
3E	$20
AE	$16

Thaddeus "Bud" Grizberg
#3202 • Original Price: $10
Issued: 1996 • Retired: 1998

④

Value	
NE	$50

**Uncle Irving Grizberg
(NALED Exclusive)**
#3204-01 • Original Price: $20
Issued: 1997 • Retired: 1997

⑤

Values	
1E	$48
2E	$32
3E	$24
AE	$17

Virginia "Ginny" Grizberg
#3210 • Original Price: $17
Issued: 1998 • Current

THE SHOE BOX BEARS

	Date Purchased	Price Paid	Value Of My Collection
1.			
2.			
3.			
4.			
5.			
PENCIL TOTALS			

SHOE BOX BEARS

(1)

Values	
1E	$45
2E	$34
3E	$25
AE	$20

Winnie Hopkins & Bunnylove
#3207 • Original Price: $20
Issued: 1998 • Current

DESK ANIMALS

The fanciful DeskAnimals grow to a menagerie of ten pieces this year, including an exclusive set from QVC, with the addition of four new pieces, including a terrific turtle, a fabulous frog and of course, the legendary Loch Ness Monster. An unusual and fun assortment of desk accessories, these animals will accentuate any flat surface just swimmingly!

(2)

Value	
NE	$11

"Bob" Moosioswimius
#380001 • Original Price: $11
Issued: 1998 • Current

THE SHOE BOX BEARS

	Date Purchased	Price Paid	Value Of My Collection
1.			

DESK ANIMALS

2.			
3.			
✏ PENCIL TOTALS			

(3)

Value	
NE	$11

"Lucy" Tigerocious Mommius
#380004 • Original Price: $11
Issued: 1998 • Current

① **Value**
NE $11

"Mel" Otterrificus
#380003 • Original Price: $11
Issued: 1998 • Current

② New! **Value**
NE $11

Puff Lochlegend
#380008 • Original Price: $11
Issued: 1999 • Current

③ New! **Value**
NE $16

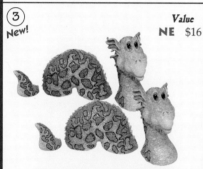

**Puff & Nessie Lochlegend
(set/2, QVC Exclusive)**
N/A • Original Price: $16
Issued: 1999 • To Be Retired: 1999

④ **Value**
NE $11

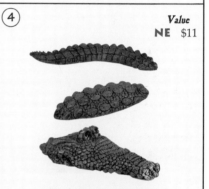

"Ray" Croccodiopius
#380000 • Original Price: $11
Issued: 1998 • Current

⑤ New! **Value**
NE $11

Shelby Turtlecrawlius
#380007 • Original Price: $11
Issued: 1999 • Current

DESK ANIMALS

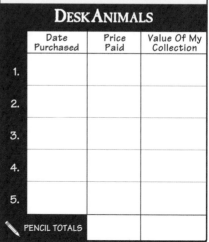

	Date Purchased	Price Paid	Value Of My Collection
1.			
2.			
3.			
4.			
5.			
✏ PENCIL TOTALS			

DESK ANIMALS

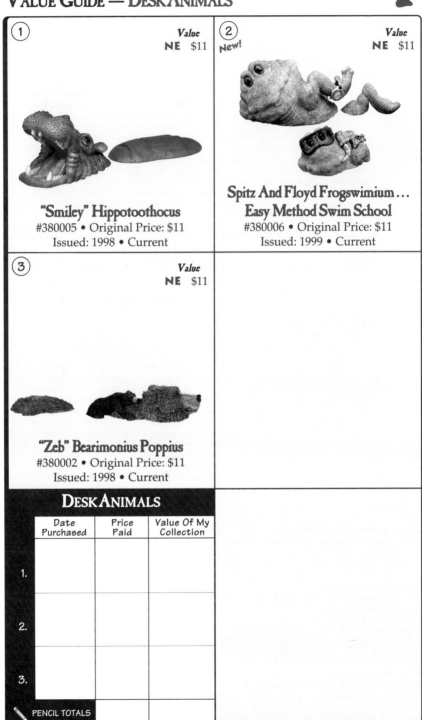

① **Value**
NE $11

"Smiley" Hippotoothocus
#380005 • Original Price: $11
Issued: 1998 • Current

② New! **Value**
NE $11

**Spitz And Floyd Frogswimium…
Easy Method Swim School**
#380006 • Original Price: $11
Issued: 1999 • Current

③ **Value**
NE $11

"Zeb" Bearimonius Poppius
#380002 • Original Price: $11
Issued: 1998 • Current

DESK ANIMALS

	Date Purchased	Price Paid	Value Of My Collection
1.			
2.			
3.			
PENCIL TOTALS			

THE LOYAL ORDER OF FRIENDS OF BOYDS

The proud members of the Boyds collector's club (a.k.a. F.o.B.s) are the lucky recipients of special club kits that include product listings, dealer directories, a subscription to the official newsletter and many surprises. Club members also have the opportunity to purchase exclusive club pieces. The club celebrates 1999 with a blooming offer of hope, joy and love.

① NEW! **Value** NE N/E

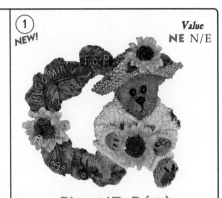

Bloomin' F.o.B. (pin)
#01999-11 • Membership Gift
Issued: 1999 • To Be Retired: 1999

② NEW! **Value** NE N/E

Blossum B. Berriweather... Bloom With Joy!
#01999-21 • Membership Gift
Issued: 1999 • To Be Retired: 1999

③ **Value** NE N/E

Eleanor
#01998-31 • Membership Gift
Issued: 1998 • Retired: 1998

④ NEW! **Value** NE N/E

Flora Mae Berriweather
#01999-31 • Membership Gift
Issued: 1999 • To Be Retired: 1999

MEMBERSHIP PIECES

	Date Purchased	Price Paid	Value Of My Collection
1.			
2.			
3.			
4.			
PENCIL TOTALS			

①

Value
NE N/E

Lady Libearty (pin)
#01998-11 • Membership Gift
Issued: 1998 • Retired: 1998

②

Value
NE N/E

Lady Libearty
#01998-21 • Membership Gift
Issued: 1998 • Retired: 1998

③

Value
NE N/E

Ms. Berriweather's Cottage
#01998-41 • Original Price: $21
Issued: 1998 • Retired: 1998

④ New!

Value
NE $11.50

Noah's Genius At Work Table
Noah's Pageant Series
#2429 • Original Price: $11.50
Issued: 1999 • To Be Retired: 1999

MEMBERSHIP PIECES

	Date Purchased	Price Paid	Value Of My Collection
1.			
2.			
3.			
4.			
5.			
PENCIL TOTALS			

⑤ New!

Value
NE $25

Plant With Hope, Grow With Love, Bloom With Joy
#01999-51 • Original Price: $25
Issued: 1999 • To Be Retired: 1999

Value
NE $30

Raeburn
#01996-31 • Membership Gift
Issued: 1996 • Retired: 1997

New!

Value
NE $23

**Sunny And Sally Berriweather...
Plant With Hope**
#01999-41 • Original Price: $23
Issued: 1999 • To Be Retired: 1999

Value
NE $22

Uncle Elliot (pin)
#01996-11 • Membership Gift
Issued: 1996 • Retired: 1997

Value
NE $80

**Uncle Elliot...
The Head Bean Wants You**
#01996-21 • Membership Gift
Issued: 1996 • Retired: 1997

Value
NE $60

Velma Q. Berriweather
#01996-51 • Original Price: $29
Issued: 1997 • Retired: 1997

MEMBERSHIP PIECES

	Date Purchased	Price Paid	Value Of My Collection
1.			
2.			
3.			
4.			
5.			
PENCIL TOTALS			

①

Value
NE $67

Velma Q. Berriweather...
The Cookie Queen

#01996-41 • Original Price: $19
Issued: 1997 • Retired: 1997

②

Value
NE N/E

Zelma G. Berriweather

#01998-51 • Original Price: $32
Issued: 1998 • Retired: 1998

MEMBERSHIP PIECES

	Date Purchased	Price Paid	Value Of My Collection
1.			
2.			
PENCIL TOTALS			

Use these pages to record future Boyds releases.

THE BEARSTONE COLLECTION	Orig. Price	Status	Market Value 1E	2E	3E	AE	Price Paid	Value Of My Collection
Twas The Night Before Xmas 228/34 9E/2820							Gift	
Merry Xmas - Ornament L080							Gift	
Stuffed Bears -								
1. Momma Mc Bear Delmar		9-14-99					Gift	
2. Baby Bear - Blue/Cream - tie, heart & pads on feet		99					Gift	
Pillow -								
1. Boyd's Bears Afternoon Tea - SP 0154							Gift	
							PENCIL TOTALS	
							PRICE PAID	MARKET VALUE

FUTURE RELEASES

Use these pages to record future Boyds releases.

THE FOLKSTONE COLLECTION	Orig. Price	Status	Market Value				Price Paid	Value Of My Collection
			1E	2E	3E	AE		
PENCIL TOTALS							Price Paid	Market Value

Use these pages to record future Boyds releases.

THE DOLLSTONE COLLECTION	Orig. Price	Status	Market Value				Price Paid	Value Of My Collection
			1E	2E	3E	AE		
The Hearth + Home Series No 3	23.00				✓		21.00	Gave To ma 10-00
3E/1006 # 3554 Barbara Ann w/Jodi & Anne Stitched w/ Love								
Kimberly & Klaus	18.00						16.00	gave to ma for Xmas -00
#3547		6E/873						
THE SHOE BOX BEARS								
DESK ANIMALS								
COLLECTOR'S CLUB PIECES								
	PENCIL TOTALS						Price Paid	Market Value

TOTAL VALUE OF MY COLLECTION

Record the value of your collection here by adding the pencil totals from the bottom of each value guide page.

THE BEARSTONE COLLECTION			THE BEARSTONE COLLECTION		
Page Number	Price Paid	Market Value	Page Number	Price Paid	Market Value
Page 47			Page 75		
Page 48			Page 76		
Page 49			Page 77		
Page 50			Page 78		
Page 51			Page 79		
Page 52			Page 80		
Page 53			Page 81		
Page 54			Page 82		
Page 55			Page 83		
Page 56			Page 84		
Page 57			Page 85		
Page 58			Page 86		
Page 59			Page 87		
Page 60			Page 88		
Page 61			Page 89		
Page 62			Page 90		
Page 63			Page 91		
Page 64			Page 92		
Page 65			Page 93		
Page 66			Page 94		
Page 67			Page 95		
Page 68			Page 96		
Page 69			Page 97		
Page 70			Page 98		
Page 71			Page 99		
Page 72			Page 100		
Page 73			Page 175		
Page 74					
TOTAL			TOTAL		

TOTAL VALUE OF MY COLLECTION

*Record the value of your collection here by adding the
pencil totals from the bottom of each value guide page.*

THE FOLKSTONE COLLECTION			THE FOLKSTONE COLLECTION		
Page Number	Price Paid	Market Value	Page Number	Price Paid	Market Value
Page 101			Page 124		
Page 102			Page 125		
Page 103			Page 126		
Page 104			Page 127		
Page 105			Page 128		
Page 106			Page 129		
Page 107			Page 130		
Page 108			Page 131		
Page 109			Page 132		
Page 110			Page 133		
Page 111			Page 134		
Page 112			Page 135		
Page 113			Page 136		
Page 114			Page 137		
Page 115			Page 138		
Page 116			Page 139		
Page 117			Page 140		
Page 118			Page 141		
Page 119			Page 142		
Page 120			Page 143		
Page 121			Page 144		
Page 122			Page 145		
Page 123			Page 146		
			Page 147		
			Page 176		
TOTAL			TOTAL		

TOTAL VALUE OF MY COLLECTION

*Record the value of your collection here by adding the
pencil totals from the bottom of each value guide page.*

THE DOLLSTONE COLLECTION			THE SHOE BOX BEARS		
Page Number	Price Paid	Market Value	Page Number	Price Paid	Market Value
Page 148			Page 165		
Page 149			Page 166		
Page 150			Page 167		
Page 151			Page 168		
Page 152			Page 177		
Page 153			TOTAL		
Page 154			DESK ANIMALS		
Page 155			Page Number	Price Paid	Market Value
Page 156			Page 168		
Page 157			Page 169		
Page 158			Page 170		
Page 159			Page 177		
Page 160			TOTAL		
Page 161			COLLECTOR'S CLUB PIECES		
Page 162			Page Number	Price Paid	Market Value
Page 163			Page 171		
Page 164			Page 172		
Page 177			Page 173		
			Page 174		
			Page 177		
TOTAL			TOTAL		

	GRAND TOTALS		
		PRICE PAID	MARKET VALUE

*W*hether you've caught the Boyds collecting bug or you're looking for an entertaining investment strategy, you might be tempted to hunt for every piece in the line. And because many pieces have been retired, tracking them down may send you on a wild goose chase. While you're searching through the collectibles wilderness for those pieces that got away, there is one stone that you should not leave unturned – the secondary market. The secondary market can be a useful tool in locating those evasive pieces, but bear in mind that when exploring it, there are several factors you should know about.

RETIREMENTS

Once a piece is honored with the status of retirement and is no longer available through regular retail outlets, it is quickly placed onto the secondary market, its value increases and the hunt commences. However, unlike many collectible lines, The Boyds Collection Ltd. announces future retirements. This strategy encourages collectors to plan their Boyds shopping, allowing them the opportunity to purchase these pieces before they become scarce.

EDITION NUMBERS

What was only intended to be a method of inventory control has become quite a phenomenon in the Boyds secondary market. Each of the resin figurines and many of the other resin pieces have "edition" numbers written on the bottom. This is Boyds' way of keeping track of how many pieces have been produced. All Bearstone (with the exception of the series which have 7,200 piece editions) and Folkstone (whose series have 9,600 piece editions) figurines have 3,600 pieces in each edition, while Dollstones have

4,800 pieces per edition, and Shoe Box Bears boast 6,000 figurines in each edition group. These editions are denoted with "1E" (first edition), "2E" (second edition) and so on. With the edition information, a second number appears which identifies the piece's production number. For example, a Bearstone figurine which has the number "1E/150" is the 150th piece produced in the first group of 3,600 figurines of that design. There is no significant difference between pieces in any edition so collectors have made these early pieces the most coveted. And to add to the challenge of finding these pieces, Boyds often produces them in large quantities – there can be more than 20 editions of a given piece – which are distributed in a random fashion to retailers across the country.

Another interesting phenomenon is the increased value of the Premier Edition, a figurine that makes its debut on the home shopping network QVC and is marked as such. Although there is rarely a difference between this edition and the one released in the regular line, it is the premier that typically has the higher value on the secondary market.

CONDITION

All observant shoppers know that if an item is damaged in any way, it's not worth as much as one in perfect condition. The sweater that is on the reduced rack with a pulled stitch or the pants with a broken zipper are better buys, if you are handy with a needle and thread. Likewise, a Boyds resin piece that has been damaged can be repaired, but upon resale the prospective buyer should be made aware that the piece being purchased has been restored.

Another factor which affects the value of a piece is the presence (or absence) of the original container or box in which the piece was shipped to the retailer. This packaging has evolved into an important resale point that will increase the value of the piece, especially on the secondary market. Pieces sold without boxes or with mismatched and incorrectly labeled boxes will be worth less than those sold with a box in perfect condition with the identifying label matching the name of the resin piece.

THE SECONDARY MARKET SCENE

Now that you know what can affect the value of your pieces, you'll need directions to the market. There are a variety of resources that you can utilize, and you should look carefully at all of them in order to select the best method for you. While some people prefer having a "face-to-face" meeting with a trusted and recommended collector, many collectors have discovered that the Internet is a wonderful new way to reach collectors that would otherwise be out of their realm.

THE INS AND OUTS OF THE INTERNET

One of the most effective, efficient and exciting secondary market resources for collectors is the Internet. This new electronic mode of communication offers everyone from the beginner to the seasoned veteran a wide variety of information and resources (which can be updated instantaneously) at the touch of a mouse! The Internet offers convenience (you don't have to fight traffic or wait until the baby wakes from her nap!), fast results, secure shopping, a vast source of information and a chance to meet like-minded collectors and establish a bond in that special "Boyds" way.

For those looking for a specific piece to buy, bulletin boards and chat rooms on a variety of Boyds-related web sites offer collectors the opportunity to contact others with the same mission – to find that "impossible to find"

bear in the haystack . . . and to experience the thrill when they do (which some Boyds collectors commonly refer to as a "YA YA!").

In addition, collectors can choose to turn to other avenues within the Internet to conduct their Boyds "buying business." Many retail stores now have their own web sites where Boyds items are offered for sale. Orders are taken and transactions are conducted with the touch of a few keys. The home shopping network, QVC, also offers the convenience and luxury of buying Boyds electronically. Internet auction sites (such as *eBay*) provide a convenient method of browsing and shopping for items that are available. However, in the midst of this convenience and the plethora of options available, you should always be careful in your purchasing strategy. Remember – you're doing this for fun!

EXCHANGES, ETC.

Another method to consider is to contact a secondary market exchange service. You can look for these exchanges in collectible magazines or on the Internet. If you prefer to deal with a "live" person, your local retailer is a good place to start. He or she may not deal directly in the secondary market but may be able to put you in touch with someone that does. If you choose an exchange service, you will find a listing of pieces that collectors wish to buy or sell and the asking price. The exchange publishes this list monthly or even daily and distributes this information to those who have purchased a subscription or paid a membership fee.

Another way to reach Boyds collectors, especially in your immediate locale, is through your hometown newspaper's classified advertisement section. To reach a more specific group of collectors, however, you might have better luck looking in the "swap & sell" sections of collectible newsletters and magazines.

EXCHANGES, DEALERS AND NEWSLETTERS

BOYDS BEAR RETAIL INQUIRER
P.O. Box 4385
Gettysburg, PA 17325
(general Boyds information written by the Head Bean Hisself; check your local store for copies!)

BEAR TALES & TRAILS
Harry Croft
518 N. Everett Drive
Palatine, IL 60067-4110
(847) 358-6276
beartales@pipeline.com

COLLECTIBLE EXCHANGE, INC.
6621 Columbiana Road
New Middletown, OH 44442
(216) 542-9646

DONNA'S COLLECTIBLES EXCHANGE
703 Endeavor Drive South
Winter Springs, FL 32708
1-800-480-5105
www.donnascollexch.com

THE FORBEARS COLLECTIBLES
David & Sandi Goerzen
297 E. Mill Avenue
Porterville, CA 93257-3935
(559) 781-1205
theforbears@ocsnet.net

ED & JANET HYMES
Edlen Estates
Lot 104
Jacksonville, IL 62650
(dealer only)

LIONS, TIGERS, AND BOYDS, OH, MY!!!
Laurie Anne Greez
P.O. Box 1393
Easton, MA 02334-1393
(newsletter only)

NEW ENGLAND COLLECTIBLES EXCHANGE
Bob Dorman
201 Pine Avenue
Clarksburg, MA 01247
(413) 663-3643
nece@collectiblesbroker.com
www.collectiblesbroker.com

oPINions
Joanne Libke
117 Twin Brooks Cove
Edmonton, Alberta, Canada
T6J-6T1
(780) 436-3120
josclans@connect.ab.ca
(a guide to Boyds pins)

MARY JO TRUAX
P.O. Box 273
101 So. First Street
Ridgeview, SD 57652

VARIATIONS

*A*uthenticity is a Boyds buzzword. Boyds creator, Gary Lowenthal warns: "Don't Buy Bears From Strangers. You Don't Know Where They've Been." But when inspecting a piece in anticipation of "the buy," a collector may notice a difference between the piece in his hand and the one left on the shelf. This is where information about variations becomes important.

Variations can occur for a number of reasons. Since the pieces are hand-made and hand-painted, the contrasts between two pieces of the same design may be due to human error, while others may be the result of changes to the actual production mold. No matter what causes the variation, always keep in mind that not all differences command a higher secondary market value. This section, however, highlights a few of the accepted valuable variations.

BEARSTONE VARIATIONS

Bailey Bear With Suitcase (#2000): The more common version of this piece has a white bottom and its texture is rough, raised and detailed. A variation of this figurine can be found with a smoother surface displaying more vibrant colors. There have been reports of 11,000 pieces of the variation, all with edition marks of 1E.

Variation

Standard Version

Bailey ... In The Orchard (#2006): The mark of Bearstone authenticity, a tiny paw print, was originally located on this piece's apple cider jug. After production of about 22 editions, the paw print was moved to Bailey's dress.

Bailey the Baker ... With Sweetie Pie (#2254): For the Teddy Bear Festival that was held in June 1995, 3,600 pieces of the "Clarion Bear" were produced. This version donned a special blue-bodiced outfit and pink head bow, and is holding a pie which has the words "CLARION . . . IOWA" baked into its top crust.

Standard Version

Variation

Byron & Chedda With Catmint (#2010): A number of minor changes occurred over the lifespan of this piece including design changes on the base as well as on the gold neck scarf. A patch on Byron's arm and stitches on his hat were added by the time third editions were produced.

Standard Version

Variation

Edmund The Elf Bear ... Holiday Glow (#2772, Votive Holder): On some pieces, the phrase "It Was The Night Before Christmas" appeared as "I Was The Night Before Christmas."

VARIATIONS

Elliot ... The Hero (#2280): On a number of these figurines, the word "Bearstone" is incorrectly spelled as "Beatstone" in the information found on its underside.

Grenville & Beatrice ... Best Friends (#2016): The dove that appears with these two bruin buddies seems to flit about, since it appears on the front center of the base of some figurines and on the right side of the base on others.

Standard Version

Variation

Grenville & Neville ... The Sign (#2099): The standard version of this piece has a white bottom, but variations showing a brown underside have been found.

Standard Version

Variation

Moriarty – The Bear In The Cat Suit (#2005): The 1993 copyright year was positioned on the side of the base in this figurine's earlier editions. On subsequent pieces, in which Moriarty's hood and cuffs are also larger, the date appears on the top of the base.

Standard Version

Variation

Ms. Griz ... Monday Morning (#2276):
This fashion-conscious
bear is quite aware that
a lady should not
wear the same outfit
too many times.
Consequently, after
about six editions,
Ms. Griz's changed
her outfit from a pink
number to a more sub-
dued, blue-green dress, with a
switch in head bows as well.

Standard Version

Variation

**Simone de Bearvoire & Her Mom,
My Auntie Alice (#2001):**
Later versions of this
"mother/daughter"
piece evolved into
a more detailed
interpretation,
including additions
of patches on the
larger bear's paws.

Standard Version

Variation

SAN FRANCISCO MUSIC BOX VARIATIONS

Boyds Arthur On Trunk (#2751SF): Arthur apparently required a
bit more packing space and, as a result, his travel case was
enlarged. His scarf also gained some tassels along with the
fringes.

Boyds Ted & Teddy (#2701SF): Later editions of this music box
were downsized from the early, larger versions.

VARIATIONS

Boyds Wilson With Love Sonnets (#2750SF): The early version of this music box featured the box, bear and books made from a one-piece mold; while in subsequent editions, the music box is made from a two-piece mold.

FOLKSTONE VARIATIONS

Beatrice ... The Birthday Angel (#2825): For some versions of this piece, Beatrice had a "growth spurt," while in others, the writing on the figurine's bow became indecipherable.

Betty Biscuit (#2824): "Betty Cocker," the piece's original name, appears only on early editions.

Florence ... The Kitchen Angel (#2824): Some early editions of this figurine can be found with the angel holding the mixing bowl by its bottom, while she is also wearing a longer skirt.

Lizzie ... The Shopping Angel (#2827): Lizzie is keeping her hand on her purse, as all careful shoppers should! She can be found either clutching the purse or just the strap. In addition, her skirt has been known to have different amounts of folds.

Minerva ... The Baseball Angel (#2826): Minerva was first found with six buttons on her jersey below her belt. She seems to have visited the seamstress, however, as later editions appeared with seven.

"GRS" AND "RS" STAMPS

These special stamps appear on the bottoms of figurines which have been made from a mold that has been remade or "resculpted" into a design different from the original. This may become necessary if the first mold has a design flaw (i.e., the neck of a particular piece is too fragile and the head breaks off easily) or if the mold itself becomes unusable because of natural deterioration.

VARIATIONS

The "GRS" and "RS" initials are used as an inventory tracking system and specifically refer to the two factories in China where the pieces are made. As with most of the early editions, the original designs usually (but not always) command a higher price on the secondary market. When "GRS" pieces are numbered, they are marked starting with "1E," so pieces with the same name may have both traditional 1E and GRS 1E numbers, a trend that recently carried over to the "RS" designs.

Boyds Bears & Friends™
... With gentle hands and a warm heart ...

Edition / pc # 73E/1523
RS STYLE #2231 Clara ... the Nurse
©1993 — THE BOYDS COLLECTION LTD
HANDMADE IN CHINA

Edition / pc # ___1
RS STYLE #2231 Clara

EXCLUSIVES

Selected retailers such as syndicated catalog groups, television shopping networks and Canadian stores are distributors of a limited number of Boyds pieces that make their debut as either exclusives (which are often introduced in the regular line with minor design changes) or early releases (which possess special bottom stamps).

Standard Version

GCC Exclusive

INSURING YOUR COLLECTION

*W*hen insuring your collection, there are three major points to consider:

1. KNOW YOUR COVERAGE: Collectibles are typically included in homeowner's or renter's insurance policies. Ask your agent if your policy covers fire, theft, floods, hurricanes, earthquakes and damage or breakage from routine handling. Also, ask if your policy covers claims at "current replacement value" – the amount it would cost to replace items if they were damaged, lost or stolen – which is extremely important since the secondary market value of some pieces may well exceed their original retail price.

2. DOCUMENT YOUR COLLECTION: In the event of a loss, you will need a record of the contents and value of your collection. Ask your insurance agent what information is acceptable. Keep receipts and an inventory of your collection in a different location, such as a safe-deposit box. Include the purchase date, price paid, size, issue year, edition limit/number, special markings and secondary market value for each piece. Photographs and video footage with close-up views of each piece, including edition numbers and signatures on the bottoms, are good backups.

3. WEIGH THE RISK: To determine the coverage you need, calculate how much it would cost to replace your collection and compare it to the total amount your current policy would pay. To insure your collection for a specific dollar amount, ask your agent about adding a Personal Articles Floater or a Fine Arts Floater or "rider" to your policy, or insuring your collection under a totally separate policy. As with all insurance, you must weigh the risk of loss against the cost of additional coverage.

 ## PRODUCTION

Production

President and master of the Boyds empire, Gary Lowenthal begins production of a new piece by sketching the ideas first conceived in his head. The new piece is then brought to life in three-dimensional clay form by talented sculptors and is revised until it achieves approval to be made into a "White Ware" casting original mold.

Next, Lowenthal and his expert painters choose colors. When the final decisions have been made, the mold is readied for the production process. Multiple editions of the piece are then hand-cast and hand-painted by Boyds artists. The completed figurines are then stamped on the bottom with the piece logo, quote, item number, title, copyright date and the words "The Boyds Collection Ltd." The edition numbers are written by hand on the bottom – adding a nice personal touch!

PACKAGING

Foam and paper packing materials protect each resin piece which is shipped in its own specially designed box: The Bearstones arrive at stores in forest green boxes that are trimmed in maroon with gold printing, while Folkstones are packed in rich maroon color boxes that are trimmed in forest green with gold printing. Additionally, *The Wee Folkstones* come with their own specially designed boxes complete with a brief story about their respective categories within the series.

The Dollstones are presented in golden yellow boxes with a decorative maroon design and The Shoe Box Bears, of course, are packaged in tiny replicas of shoe boxes. Finally, the DeskAnimals are protected by brown boxes decorated with a variety of tiny paw prints.

GLOSSARY

1E — a notation on the bottom of Boyds resin figurines denoting the "first edition" pieces. These are generally the most sought-after pieces in the Boyds collection (also see **EDITION**).

2E, 3E, ETC. — notations identifying the edition number of figurines produced after the "1E" pieces.

BRONZE PAW DEALERS — the third of the three tiers of Boyds retailers who receive priority shipping and larger allotments of certain pieces.

BOTTOMSTAMP — identifying marks on the underside of Boyds resin figurines. These marks may include such information as the title, collection logo, copyright years, quote, phrase, etc.

COLLECTIBLE — anything and everything that is "able to be collected," such as figurines and dolls. Even *walking sticks* can be considered a "collectible," but it is generally recognized that a true collectible should be something that increases in value over time.

EARLY RELEASE — early release of "next year's introductions" offered to groups of retailers who participate in a selected gift catalog program.

EDITION — the numbering system used by The Boyds Collection Ltd. to keep track of the number of resin pieces produced. Typically, there are 3,600 pieces for Bearstone and Folkstone editions, 4,800 pieces per Dollstone edition and 6,000 pieces per Shoe Box Bear edition.

EXCHANGE — a secondary market service that lists pieces that collectors wish to buy or sell. The exchange works as a middleman and may require a commission.

EXCLUSIVE — a figurine made especially for, and available only through, a specific store, buying group or wholesaler.

GIFT CREATIONS CONCEPTS (GCC) — a syndicated catalog group with more than 300 retail stores nationwide. Exclusive pieces and early releases are commonly available through these retailers.

GOLD PAW DEALERS — the highest tier of Boyds retailers who receive priority shipping and larger allotments of certain pieces.

GRS — a notation identifying Boyds resin pieces that have been made from a "resculpted" mold. This mark is also seen as "RS."

INTERNATIONAL COLLECTIBLE EXPOSITION — a national collectible show held annually in June in Rosemont, Illinois and in April alternating between Edison, New Jersey and Long Beach, California.

ISSUE PRICE — the retail price of an item when it is first introduced.

JOINTED — describes a piece whose arms, legs or head move.

LAUNCH — the debut of a piece on the home shopping channel QVC. These pieces are usually released to stores in the following months.

LIMITED EDITION (LE) — a piece scheduled for a predetermined production quantity or time. (Ex. "Gary, Tina, Matt & Bailey . . . From Our Home To Yours" is limited to 1999 production).

MINT CONDITION — a piece offered on the secondary market that is in like-new condition. "Mint in box" means the piece comes in its original box.

NALED (NATIONAL ASSOCIATION OF LIMITED EDITION DEALERS) — a retail trade association. Exclusive pieces and early releases are commonly available through these retailers.

OPEN EDITION — a piece with no predetermined limitation on the time or size of the production run.

PREMIER EDITION — the edition marking given to pieces originally introduced and sold on QVC.

PRIMARY MARKET — the conventional collectibles purchasing process in which collectors buy directly from dealers at issue price.

RETIRED — a piece that is taken out of production, never to be made again. This is usually followed by a scarcity of the piece and an increase in value on the secondary market.

RS — a notation identifying Boyds resin pieces that have been made from a "resculpted" mold. This mark is also seen as "GRS."

SECONDARY MARKET — the source for buying and selling collectibles according to basic supply-and-demand principles ("pay what the market will bear"). Popular pieces that are sold out or have been retired can appreciate in value far above the original issue price. Pieces are sold through newspaper ads, collector newsletters, the Internet and "swap & sells" at collector gatherings.

SILVER PAW DEALERS — the second of the three tiers of Boyds retailers who receive priority shipping and larger allotments of certain pieces.

SUDDEN DEATH RETIREMENT — the sudden, "unplanned" removal of a piece from production (at the discretion of the "Head Bean"). Pieces designated as sudden death retirements are retired as soon as the stock runs out. Typically, Boyds retirements are announced in advance.

SWAP & SELL — event where collectors meet to buy, sell or trade items.

VARIATIONS — pieces that have color, design or printed text changes from the "original" piece, whether intentional or not. Some are minor changes, while some are important enough to affect the piece's value on the secondary market.

– Key –

All Boyds resin pieces are listed below in numerical order by item number. The first number refers to the piece's location within the Value Guide section and the second to the box in which it is pictured on that page.

Item	Page #	Pict #
BC2050	65	5
BC2051	54	2
BC2066	65	3
BC2210	62	5
BC2228	58	5
BC22851	53	4
BC35031	149	4
BC36507	132	1
BC94281	100	5
BC361021	127	5
2000	49	4
2001	70	3
2002	68	2
2004	72	2
2005	67	2
2006	50	1
2007	73	2
2008	59	1
2010	52	5
2011	55	4
2012	54	1
2014	51	4
2015	64	1
2016	60	2
2017	49	2
2018	49	1
2019	70	1
2030	61	2
2099	60	5
2222	72	5
2223	71	2
2225	62	4
2226	55	5

Item	Page #	Pict #
2227	69	5
2229	53	3
2230	53	2
2231	54	3
2233	61	1
2235	64	4
2236	57	2
2237	55	2
2238	66	4
2239	52	2
2240	56	4
2241	57	5
2242	57	4
2243	66	2
2245	64	3
2246	47	1
2247	63	2
2250	55	1
2251	55	3
2251SF	93	1
2253	65	2
2254	50	3
2255	60	4
2258	47	4
2259	67	3
2260	51	3
2261	73	1
2262	68	4
2263	71	5
2265	61	3
2266	48	1
2267	70	2
2268	51	1
2269	58	4
2272	49	5
2273	64	2
2274	60	3
2275	66	1
2276	67	4
2277	58	3
2278	68	3
2279	70	4
2280	58	1
2281	61	5
2282	67	1
2283	64	5

Item	Page #	Pict #
2284	67	5
2286	73	3
2401	75	3
2402	76	3
2403	74	1
2404	76	4
2405	74	5
2406	75	4
2407	76	2
2408	74	4
2409	76	5
2410	74	2
2411	73	4
2412	74	3
2414	75	2
2415	75	1
2416	75	5
2425	76	1
2426	77	2
2427	77	1
2428	77	4
2429	172	4
2450	77	3
2500	82	3
2501	82	5
2502	81	3
2505	81	5
2506	83	4
2507	82	2
2508	83	5
2550	139	4
2551	139	5
2552	141	3
2553	137	4
2560	140	1
2561	138	2
2562	138	4
2563	142	1
2564	137	3
2565	141	5
2600	99	5
2601	98	16
2603	99	4
2604	97	8
2605	96	7
2606	98	2

Item	Page #	Pict #
2607	99	12
2608	97	5
2609	100	4
2610	99	17
2611	97	13
2612	96	5
2614	99	1
2615	97	6
2616	96	4
2617	97	7
2618	98	10
2619	98	14
2625	145	2
2631	97	17
2632	98	3
2634	96	12
2635	96	1
2636	97	19
2638	144	10
2639	99	13
2642	97	18
2647	145	19
2648	146	6
2649	146	8
2650	146	5
2651	145	12
2652	147	8
2653	147	2
2658	145	18
2661	144	15
2662	98	13
2663	96	6
2664	144	11
2665	147	6
2666	144	1
2667	96	17
2668	144	13
2669	146	16
2671	144	3
2674	146	11
2679	99	14
2700	90	1
2701SF	95	4
2702	89	1
2703	143	4
2704	89	3

Page #	Pict #	Page #	Pict #	Page #	Pict #	Page #	Pict #
2705 90	4	2814 117	1	2871 121	1	3518 148	2
2706 90	3	2815 110	1	2872 101	2	3519 155	3
2710 143	2	2816 119	2	2873 103	5	3520 152	3
2711SF . . . 164	5	2817 115	5	2874 120	3	3521 158	1
2720 164	1	2818 108	4	2875 108	2	3522 153	4
2750SF 95	5	2819 117	3	2880 . . . 118	2	3523 158	2
2751SF 91	1	2820 101	3	2881 111	3	3524 149	3
2752SF 93	3	2821 101	4	2882 117	4	3525 150	1
2753SF 92	4	2822 102	1	2883 114	2	3526 155	5
2754SF 94	5	2823 117	2	2899 120	4	3527 157	1
2755SF 91	4	2824 108	1			3529 148	3
2756SF 94	4	2825 103	3	3000 126	1	3530 151	3
2757SF 91	2	2826 113	2	3001 125	3	3531 157	3
2758SF 95	3	2827 111	4	3002 125	4	3532 152	2
2759SF 90	5	2828 120	1	3003 125	2	3533 156	4
2761SF 94	1	2829 101	1	3004 126	2	3534 149	2
2762SF 92	5	2830 110	3	3200 165	1	3535 153	5
2763SF 91	5	2831 104	3	3201 166	1	3536 154	1
2764SF 95	2	2832 113	1	3202 167	3	3537 154	5
2765SF 93	2	2833 109	2	3203 166	3	3538 151	2
2767SF 91	3	2834 118	4	3205 167	1	3539 148	1
2768SF 95	1	2835 106	4	3206 165	2	3540 157	2
2769SF 94	2	2836 103	4	3207 168	1	3541 155	1
2770 87	5	2837 106	1	3208 165	4	3542 153	2
2770SF 93	4	2838 121	5	3209 166	4	3599 148	4
2771 87	4	2839 113	4	3210 167	5	3600 129	1
2772 87	3	2840 115	1	3211 166	5		
2772SF 93	5	2841 118	1	3212 165	3	4900 161	4
2773SF 92	1	2842 110	2	3214 167	2	4901 163	1
2775SF . . . 164	4	2843 107	5	3500 152	1	4902 160	4
2776SF . . . 164	3	2844 104	5	3501 155	4	4903 162	3
2777SF 92	3	2845 121	2	3502 157	4	4904 160	2
2778SF 92	2	2846 107	4	3503 149	5	4905 162	5
2800 116	1	2847 118	3	3504 154	4	4906 160	3
2801 116	4	2848 113	3	3505 153	1	4907 162	1
2802 116	2	2849 115	2	3506 149	1	4908 161	1
2803 120	5	2850 119	3	3507 156	3	4909 163	2
2804 115	4	2851 106	2	3508 151	1	4910 161	5
2805 116	5	2852 109	3	3509 156	1	4912 161	3
2806 116	3	2853 106	3	3510 151	4	4914 162	4
2807 115	3	2854 111	5	3511 155	2	4915 160	5
2808 119	4	2860 107	1	3512 150	3		
2809 117	5	2865 118	5	3514 150	2	25650 140	2
2810 121	4	2866 119	1	3515GCC . 152	5	25651 137	5
2811 105	1	2868 102	4	3516 153	3	25653 139	1
2812 110	4	2870 104	1	3517 154	2	25653GCC 138	5

Page #	Pict #	Page #	Pict #	Page #	Pict #	Page #	Pict #
25654 137	1	26020 100	3	26314 146	14	27721 88	1
25655 140	4	26021 97	15	26315 146	17	27722 87	1
25700 82	1	26022 96	2	26316 147	4	27723 86	5
25701 81	4	26023 100	2	26317 144	6	27745SF . . . 94	3
25702 85	2	26100 98	12	26318 145	9	27750 87	2
25703 80	5	26101 100	1	26319 144	2	27751 88	3
25704 84	4	26102 97	3	26320 147	1	27752 86	4
25705 83	2	26103 97	10	26321 146	12	27753 88	5
25706 83	3	26104 96	16	26400 145	3	27754 88	4
25707 82	4	26105 96	18	26401 146	2	27800 143	1
25708 81	1	26106 97	1	26402 144	16	27801 142	5
25709 84	3	26107 96	11	26403 144	12	27802 142	4
25710 81	2	26108 97	2	26404 144	7	27803 142	3
25711 84	5	26109 97	4	26405 146	1	27900 163	4
25712 83	1	26110 98	17	26406 145	15	27950 163	5
25800 140	3	26111 99	3	26407 146	4	27951 163	3
25850 160	1	26112 98	9	26408 146	10	28001 103	2
25851 159	4	26114 98	18	26409 145	16	28002 107	3
25852 159	5	26115 98	6	26410 147	5	28101 104	4
25900 139	2	26116 98	20	26411 145	4	28102 109	1
25950 138	1	26117 96	13	26412 144	18	28201 105	3
25951GCC . 85	3	26118 96	15	26414 145	6	28202 102	4
25952GCC . 84	1	26119 99	9	26415 145	5	28203 109	5
25953 84	2	26120 99	2	26416 146	3	28204 120	2
25954 80	4	26121 96	10	26417 145	11	28205 105	2
25955 85	1	26122 97	9	26418 145	1	28206 111	1
25956 139	3	26123 96	3	26419 146	15	28207 112	2
25990 80	3	26124 99	16	26420 145	20	28240 112	4
26001 97	20	26125 99	19	26421 144	5	28241 114	3
26002 98	1	26126 97	12	26422 145	10	28242 103	1
26003 97	14	26127 97	11	26423 145	8	28243 112	3
26004 97	16	26128 98	11	26562 136	4	28244 114	1
26005 98	4	26129 99	10	27300 79	4	28245 104	2
26006 98	19	26300 146	7	27301 78	4	28246 113	5
26007 99	15	26301 147	3	27302 79	1	28247 114	4
26008 98	15	26302 145	13	27350 79	3	28249 105	4
26009 98	8	26303 144	4	27351 78	3	28401 121	3
26010 98	7	26304 144	17	27353 79	2	28402 108	3
26011 99	20	26305 146	13	27354 78	2	28428 111	2
26012 96	9	26306 145	14	27402 135	3		
26014 99	6	26307 145	17	27450 135	4	3528-1 156	2
26015 98	5	26308 144	14	27451 135	2	36002 130	5
26016 96	14	26309 145	7	27550 158	4	36003 129	3
26017 99	11	26310 146	9	27551 158	3	36004 131	4
26018 99	18	26311 144	9	27600 78	1	36100 126	3
26019 96	8	26312 147	7	27720 88	2	36101 130	3

Page #	Pict #	Page #	Pict #	Page #	Pict #	Page #	Pict #
36102.....128	1	227702.....68	1	272001....159	3	380006....170	2
36103.....128	4	227703.....63	3	272052....159	1	380007....169	5
36104.....132	3	227704.....50	2	272053....164	2	380008....169	2
36105.....127	4	227705.....65	4	272054....159	2		
36106.....129	4	227706.....52	4	281035SYN. 109	4	654281GCC 86	1
36201.....127	2	227707.....54	5			654282GCC 85	4
36300.....128	2	227708.....58	2	3201-01...166	2	654291.....86	2
36301.....128	3	227709.....66	3	3204-01...167	4		
36302.....130	1	227710.....59	2	3210-01...151	5	01996-11..173	4
36303.....131	1	227711.....66	5	3512-01...150	4	01996-21..173	4
36304.....127	1	227712.....50	4	3515-01...152	4	01996-31..173	1
36305.....130	2	227714.....48	2	3531-01...154	3	01996-41..174	1
36400.....132	2	227715GCC. 56	1	36501-1...131	3	01996-51..173	5
36401.....128	5	227717.....53	5	370000....124	1	01997-71...69	1
36402GCC. 130	4	227718.....52	3	370001....122	1	01998-11..172	1
36500.....131	5	227719.....72	3	370002....122	3	01998-21..172	2
36501.....131	2	227720.....47	2	370003....123	4	01998-31..171	3
36502.....129	5	227721.....59	3	370004....124	3	01998-41..172	3
36503.....127	3	227722GCC. 53	1	370050....123	3	01998-51..174	2
36504.....129	2	227801.....59	4	370051....124	5	01998-71...57	3
36505.....126	4	227802.....51	5	370052....125	1	01998-81...99	7
36700.....133	1	227803.....71	3	370053....123	1	01999-11..171	1
36701.....133	2	227804.....59	5	370054....123	2	01999-21..171	2
36702.....133	3	2283-01.....65	1	370100....124	2	01999-31..171	4
36703.....134	2	228302.....71	1	370101....122	2	01999-41..173	2
36704.....133	4	228303.....63	4	370102....122	4	01999-51..172	5
36705.....133	5	228304.....48	4	370103....123	5	01999-71...72	1
36750.....134	1	228305.....69	2	370104....124	4		
36751.....132	4	228306.....60	1	370200....141	1	28203-06..107	2
63711.....138	3	228307.....69	3	370201....136	5	28206-06..102	2
63714.....141	4	228308.....62	2	370202....137	2	28207-06..112	1
65427.....142	2	228309.....56	2	370203....140	5		
65428GCC . 85	5	228310.....69	4	370204....141	2	227701-07..57	1
65429.....86	3	228311.....56	5	370300....136	2	227701-10..51	2
		228312.....56	3	370301....135	1		
94575POG . 52	1	228314GCC. 47	3	370302....136	1		
94577POG . 63	1	270501.....79	5	370500....146	19		
		270550.....90	2	370501....144	8		
2003-03....48	3	270551.....89	2	370503....146	18		
2003-04....61	4	270552.....89	4	370504....146	20		
2003-08....62	1	270553.....80	1	380000....169	4		
2020-06....72	4	270554.....80	2	380001....168	2		
2020-09....49	3	270601 89	5	380002....170	3		
2029-10....63	5	270602....143	3	380003....169	1		
2029-11....54	4	271001 ...143	5	380004....168	3		
2249-06....68	5	271050....136	3	380005....170	1		

– Key –

All Boyds resin pieces are listed below in alphabetical order. The first number refers to the piece's location within the Value Guide section and the second to the box in which it is pictured on that page.

	Page #	Pict #
1999 Canadian Exclusive Pin	100	5
Abigail . . . Peaceable Kingdom	101	1
Above The Clouds	80	3
Agatha & Shelly . . . "Scaredy Cat"	47	1
Alden & Priscilla . . . The Pilgrims	96	1
Alden . . . Trick Or Treat	96	2
Alexandra & Belle . . . "Telephone Tied"	47	2
Alexis Bearinsky . . . Twas The Night Before Christmas	47	3
Alice & Emily	144	1
Alice Spillen . . . Waitressing	96	3
Alice's Flight	96	4
Alvin T. MacBarker . . . Dog Face	101	2
Alyssa With Caroline . . . A Stitch In Time	148	1
Amazing Bailey . . . "Magic Show At 4," The	148	2
Amelia	96	5
Amelia The Bunny, Bailey With Blue Bow & Bailey With Straw Hat	100	6
Amelia The Bunny, Bailey With Blue Bow & Hop-A-Long	100	7
Amelia's Enterprise	90	5
Amelia's Enterprise . . . Carrot Juice	47	4
Amy And Edmund . . . Momma's Clothes	148	3
Angel Of Freedom	101	3
Angel Of Love	101	4
Angel Of Peace	102	1
Angelica . . . In Flight	85	4
Angelica The Angel, Bessie The Cow & Emma In Spring Bonnet	100	8
Angelica . . . The Guardian (#2266)	48	1
Angelica . . . The Guardian (#2702)	89	1
Angelica With Lily	96	6
Angelica's Flight	96	7
Angelina . . . Key To My Heart	144	2
Angelina "Smidge" Angellove . . . Angel of True Love	126	3
Anne . . . The Masterpiece	148	4
Ariel & Clarence . . . As The Pair O' Angels	73	4
Ariel . . . Love Conquers All	96	8
Ariel . . . The Guardian	144	3
Arlo In The Pumpkin Wreath	96	9
Arnold . . . Chip N' Putt	96	10
Arnold P. Bomber . . . The Duffer	48	2
Arthur On Trunk	91	1
Arthur . . . With Red Scarf	48	3
Ashley The Angel	144	4
Ashley With Chrissie . . . Dress Up	149	1
Astrid Isinglass . . . Snow Angel	102	2
Athena . . . The Wedding Angel	102	3
Audubon P. Pussywillow, The Birdwatcher (#2868)	102	4
Audubon P. Pussywillow, The Birdwatcher (#27803)	142	3
Augustus "Gus" Grizberg	165	1
Auntie Cocoa . . . Life Is Short	144	5
Auntie Cocoa M. Maximus . . . Chocolate Angel	103	1
Austin & Allen . . . The Fire Chief	149	2
Axel . . . Let It Snow	144	6
Axel . . . Thou Shalt Not Melt!	136	4
Baby Amelia's Carrot Juice	144	7
Baby's Christmas "1998"	80	4
Baby's First Christmas	80	5
Bailey & Becky . . . Diary Secrets	96	11
Bailey & Becky . . . The Diary	48	4
Bailey & Emily	91	2
Bailey & Emily . . . Forever Friends	49	1
Bailey & Emma . . . The Sisters	96	12
Bailey & Huck . . . Wheee!!!	86	4
Bailey & Matthew . . . The Gift	86	5
Bailey & Wixie . . . To Have And To Hold	49	2
Bailey At The Beach	49	3
Bailey Bear With Suitcase	49	4
Bailey . . . Birthday Wishes	96	13
Bailey . . . Born To Shop	96	14
Bailey . . . Carpe Diem	96	15
Bailey . . . Chocolate Wreath	96	16
Bailey . . . Heart's Desire	49	5
Bailey . . . Home Sweet Home	81	1
Bailey Honey Bear	91	3
Bailey In Spring Bonnet	96	17
Bailey In The Garden	96	18
Bailey . . . In The Orchard	50	1
Bailey . . . Life Is A Daring Adventure (#26106)	97	1
Bailey . . . Life Is A Daring Adventure (#27354)	78	2
Bailey . . . Love Conquers All	97	2
Bailey . . . On Time	78	1
Bailey . . . Poor Ol' Bear	50	2
Bailey . . . Tea Time	97	3
Bailey The Baker . . . With Sweetie Pie	50	3
Bailey . . . The Bride	50	4
Bailey . . . The Cheerleader	51	1
Bailey . . . The Graduate	97	4
Bailey . . . The Graduate – Carpe Diem	51	2
Bailey . . . The Honey Bear	51	3
Bailey . . . The Night Before Christmas	79	5
Bailey . . . "True Love"	78	3
Bailey With Suitcase	91	4
Bailey's Birthday (#2014)	51	4
Bailey's Birthday (#27635F)	91	5
Bailey's Bonnet	97	5
Bailey's Garden	97	6
Bailey's Springtime	97	7
Baldwin . . . As The Child	78	1
Barnaby . . . Homeward Bound (#370001)	122	1
Barnaby . . . Homeward Bound (#370101)	122	2
Barnaby . . . Homeward Bound (#370201)	136	5
Barnaby . . . Homeward Bound (#370501)	144	8
Barnaby Jr . . . Homeward Bound	122	2
Barnaby's Snow Sweep Service	135	1
Bearly Nick And Buddies	103	2
Bearly Santa	144	9
Beatrice . . . The Birthday Angel	103	3
Beatrice . . . The Giftgiver	103	4
Beatrice The Giftgiver, Clarence The Angel & Jingles The Snowman	100	9
Beatrice . . . We Are Always The Same Age Inside	51	5
Beatrice's Wreath	144	10
Bee My Honey	52	1
Benjamin With Matthew . . . The Speed Trap	149	3
Bernice As Mrs. Noah . . . Chief Cook	77	1
Bernie . . . Igotwatiwanted St. Bernard Santa	103	5
Bessie The Santa Cow	52	2
Bessie With Sun Flowers	144	11
Bessie's Chris-moo-se	97	8
Betsey And Edmund With Union Jack	149	4
Betsey With Edmund . . . The Patriots	149	5
Betsy . . . Sail Away	160	2
Betty Biscuit (#2870)	104	1
Betty Biscuit (#26403)	144	12
Birdie Holeinone . . . NQGA Of Golfers	104	2

	Page #	Pict #
Bjorn . . . With Nils & Sven	137	1
Bloomin' F.o.B.	171	1
Blossum B. Berriweather . . .		
Bloom With Joy	171	2
"Bob" Moosioswimius	168	2
Bobby . . . The Defender	126	4
Boowinkle Von Hindenmoose	104	3
Born To Shop	92	1
Bridges . . . Scuba Frog	132	4
Bristol . . . Just Sweepin'	104	4
Brittany . . . Life's Journey	160	3
Bruce . . . As The Shepherd	74	2
Bumble B. Bee . . . Sweeter Than Honey	52	3
Burt . . . Bundle Up (#370002)	122	3
Burt . . . Bundle Up (#370202)	137	2
Burt Jr . . . Bundle Up	122	4
Buster Goes a' Courtin'	104	5
Buzz . . . The Flash	52	4
Byron & Chedda With Catmint	52	5
Caffeinata (Speedy) P. Faeriebean . . .		
The Coffee Faerie	127	1
Caitlin With Emma & Edmund . . .		
Diapering Baby	150	1
Caledonia . . . As The Narrator	74	3
Candice With Matthew . . .		
Gathering Apples (#3514)	150	2
Candice With Matthew . . .		
Gathering Apples (#25851)	159	4
Caren B. Bearlove	53	1
Celeste . . . The Angel Rabbit	53	2
Celestina . . . Peace Angel	81	2
Cerebella "Smarty" Faerienoggin	127	2
Charity . . . Angel Bear With Star	81	3
Charles Dunkleburger Prince Of		
Tales . . . Kiss Me Quick!	133	1
Charlotte & Bebe . . . The Gardeners	53	3
Checkers	92	2
Chelsea Kainada . . . The Practice	53	4
Chester Bigheart . . . Love Much	123	1
Chilly & Son With Dove	105	1
Chilly With Wreath	137	3
Chrissie . . . Game, Set, Match	53	5
Chrissie . . . Tennis Anyone?	97	9
Christian By The Sea	54	1
Christmas Bear Elf With List	54	2
Cicely & Juneau . . . Iced Tea Party	127	3
Clair With Gingerbread Man	81	4
Clara . . . Get Well	97	10
Clara . . . The Nurse	54	3
Clara The Nurse	92	3
Clarence & Angelica . . . Flight Training	87	1
Clarence & Raphael . . . Angels Fly High	86	2
Clarence Angel	92	4
Clarence Angel Bear	54	4
Cocoa M. Angelrich & Scoop	136	3
Collector, The (#2762SF)	92	5
Collector, The (#27301)	78	4
Collector, The (#227707)	54	5
Collector, The (#270551)	89	2
Confidentia "No-Tell" Faeriewhisper	127	4
Constance & Felicity . . .		
Best Friend Angels	105	2
Cookie Catberg . . . Knittin' Kitten	55	1
Cookie The Santa Cat	55	2
Cosmos . . . The Gardening Angel	105	3
Courtney With Phoebe . . . Over The		
River And Thru The Woods (3512)	150	3
Courtney With Phoebe . . . Over The River		
And Thru The Woods (#3512-01)	150	4
Daffodil . . . The Colors Of Sunshine	97	11
Dahlia . . . My Biggest Blossom	97	12
Daphne And Eloise	93	1
Daphne & Eloise . . . Women's Work	55	3

	Page #	Pict #
Daphne And Eloise . . . Women's Work	80	1
Daphne Hare & Maisey Ewe	55	4
Daphne In Straw Hat	144	13
Daphne . . . In The Cabbage Patch	87	2
Daphne . . . The Reader Hare	55	5
Daphne With Dove	97	13
Darby & Jasper . . .		
Knitten' Kittens (#27451)	135	2
Darby & Jasper . . .		
Knitten' Kittens (#27802)	142	4
Dean Newbearger III . . . Bears & Bulls	56	1
December 26th	125	2
Deck The Halls	93	2
Dentinata Canadian Tooth Faerie	127	5
Dentinata "Faeriefloss" . . .		
The Tooth Faerie	128	1
Domestica T. Whirlwind . . .		
NQGA Of Super Moms	105	4
Dr. Harrison Griz . . . M.D., Ph.D., B.U.D.	56	2
Eddie . . . Proud To Be A Bearmerican	56	3
Edmund And Bailey . . . Caroling	97	14
Edmund & Bailey . . . Gathering Holly	56	4
Edmund . . . "Believe"	81	5
Edmund . . . Deck The Halls (#26021)	97	15
Edmund . . . Deck The Halls (#65428GCC)	85	3
Edmund The Elf Bear . . . Holiday Glow	87	3
Edmund The Elf . . . The Christmas Carol	56	5
Edmund . . . The Graduate —		
Carpe Diem	57	1
Edmund . . . The Night Before Christmas	79	1
Edmund The Santa Bear . . . Believe	97	16
Edmund With Wreath	82	1
Egads . . . The Skier	144	14
Egon . . . The Skier	106	1
Eleanor	171	3
"Electra" Angelbyte . . .		
Angel of Computer Training	128	2
Elgin And Elliot The Elves . . .		
Toasty Warm	87	4
Elgin The Elf Bear (#2236)	57	2
Elgin The Elf Bear (#2631)	97	17
Elias "The Elf" Grizberg	165	2
Elizabeth And Gary	150	5
Elizabeth . . . I Am The Queen	57	3
Ellie Grizberg . . . Egg Hunter	165	3
Elliot & Snowbeary	57	4
Elliot And The Lights	97	18
Elliot Bear With Jingle Bell Wreath	97	19
Elliot . . . The Fireman	97	20
Elliot . . . The Hero (#2280)	58	1
Elliot . . . The Hero (#654281GCC)	86	1
Elliot & The Tree (#2241)	57	5
Elliot & The Tree (#2704)	89	3
Elliot With Tree (#2507)	82	2
Elliot With Tree (#26002)	98	1
Elliot's Wreath	98	2
Elmer . . . Been Farmin' Long?	106	2
Elmo "Tex" Beefcake . . . On The Range	106	3
Eloise In The Cabbage Patch	144	15
Eloise . . . Tea Toter	144	16
Elvira & Chauncey Fitzbruin . . .		
Shipmates	58	2
Elvira & Chauncey . . . Shipmates	89	4
Emily . . . The Future	160	4
Emily With Kathleen & Otis . . .		
The Future (#3508)	151	1
Emily With Kathleen & Otis . . .		
The Future (#272052)	159	1
Emma & Bailey . . . Afternoon Tea	58	3
Emma & Bailey Tea Party	93	3
Emma . . . The Witchy Bear	58	4
Emma The Witchy Bear	98	3
Emma The Witchy Bear . . .		
Pumpkin Magic	87	5

	Page #	Pict #
Erin . . . Lemonade For Two	160	5
Ernest Hemmingmoose . . . The Hunter	106	4
Ernest On The Pumpkin Wreath	98	4
Esmeralda The Witch	144	17
Esmeralda . . . The Wonderful Witch	107	1
Essex . . . As The Donkey	74	4
Estudious "Cram" Faeriebaum . . . The Study Faerie	128	3
Etheral . . . Angel Of Light	107	2
Ewell & Walton . . . Manitoba Mooselmen	58	5
Execunick . . . The First Global Business Man	107	3
Faith . . . Angel Bear With Trumpet	82	3
Father Chrisbear And Son	59	1
Father Christmas	137	4
Feldman D. Finklebearg And Dooley . . . "Painless And The Patient"	59	2
Felicity Angelbliss . . . The Bride's Angel	128	4
Felicity . . . Stocking Stuffer	98	5
Fenton J. Padworthy . . . The Formal Frog	144	18
Fergus "Bogey" MacDivot	128	5
Filbert Q. Foghorn . . . The Commodore	165	4
Fixit . . . Santa's Faerie	129	1
Flakey . . . Ice Sculptor	129	2
Flash McBear	98	6
Flash McBear & The Sitting	59	3
Flora, Amelia & Eloise . . . The Tea Party	107	4
Flora & Amelia . . . The Gardeners	107	5
Flora . . . Hoppy Spring	145	1
Flora Mae Berriweather	171	4
Florence . . . The Kitchen Angel	108	1
Florence Wings It	145	2
Florina's Wreath	145	3
"Flossie" . . . Keep Smiling	145	4
Flying Lesson . . . This End Up, The (#227801)	59	4
Flying Lesson . . . This End Up, The (#270601)	89	5
Francoise & Suzanne . . . The Spree	108	2
Frogmorton And Tad . . . Fly Fishing	133	2
Frogmorton & Tad . . . Fly Fishing	135	3
Frogmorton . . . Fish, Lie, Fish	145	5
Frogmorton . . . Pad Sweet Pad	145	6
Frosty Kristabell	145	7
Gabrielle "Gabby" Faeriejabber	129	3
Garden Secrets	93	3
Gardening Friends	164	3
Gary, Tina, Matt, & Bailey . . . From Our Home To Yours	59	5
George and Gracie . . . Forever	82	2
Gertrude "Gertie" Grizberg	166	1
Gladys	166	2
Goin' To Grandma's	164	4
Grace & Faith . . . I Have A Dream	159	2
Grace & Jonathan . . . Born To Shop	60	1
Grace . . . Born To Shop	98	7
Grandma Faeriehugs	129	4
Grenville & Beatrice	93	4
Grenville & Beatrice . . . Best Friends	60	2
Grenville & Beatrice . . . True Love	60	3
Grenville & Knute . . . Football Buddies	60	4
Grenville & Neville . . . The Sign	60	5
Grenville . . . The "Flakie" Santa Bear	98	8
Grenville . . . The Graduate	61	1
Grenville The Santabear (#2030)	61	2
Grenville The Santabear (#2700)	90	1
Grenville . . . The Storyteller	61	3
Grenville . . . With Green Scarf	61	4
Grenville With Matthew & Bailey . . . Sunday Afternoon	61	5
Grenville . . . With Red Scarf	62	1
Guinevere The Angel . . . Love Is The Master Key	62	2
Gwain & Guinevere	62	3
Half Pipe . . . The Hot Dogger	129	5
Harriet & Punch With Hermaine . . . The Challenge	108	3
Harriet . . . Farm Fresh	145	8
Heart's Desire	93	5
Heath . . . As Caspar	74	5
Heather . . . Hugs And Kisses	98	9
Heather With Lauren . . . Bunny Helpers	151	2
Heavenly Wall Sconce	86	3
Helga . . . Be Warm	145	9
Helga With Ingrid & Anna . . . Be Warm	108	4
Homer	98	10
Homer On The Plate (#BC2210)	62	5
Homer On The Plate (#2225)	62	4
Homer On The Plate (#2761SF)	94	1
Homer On The Plate (#270550)	90	2
Honey B. Elfberg With Gabriella	63	1
Hop-A-Long . . . The Deputy	63	2
Hope . . . Angel Bear With Wreath	82	5
Humboldt . . . The Simple Bear	63	3
I.B. Coldman . . . Ice Is Nice	109	1
Ichabod Mooselman . . . The Pilgrim	109	2
Ida & Bessie . . . The Gardeners	109	3
Ike & Libby . . . "Stars & Stripes Forever"	109	4
Illumina . . . Angel Of Light	109	5
Immaculata Faerieburg . . . The Cleaning Faerie	130	1
Immaculata . . . Scrub-A-Dub!	145	10
Indulgenia Q. Bluit . . . Angel Of Denial	130	2
Infiniti Faerielove . . . The Wedding Faerie	130	3
Ingrid . . . Be Warm	137	5
Ingrid & Olaf . . . Be Warm	142	5
Iown Payne . . . Aerobics Angel	114	1
Iris . . . Purple Passion	98	11
J.B. & The Basketballs	98	12
Jacques Grenouille . . . The Wine Taster	133	3
Jacques . . . Starlight Skier	138	1
Jamie And Thomasina . . . The Last One	151	3
Jamie . . . The Last One (#4908)	161	1
Jamie . . . The Last One (N/A)	161	2
Jasper . . . Knittin' Kitten	145	11
Jean Claude & Jacque . . . The Skiers (#2561)	138	2
Jean Claude & Jacque . . . The Skiers (#2710)	143	2
Jean Claude & Jacque . . . The Skiers (#2815)	110	1
Jean Claude The Skier	145	12
Jean With Elliot & Debbie . . . The Bakers (#3510)	151	4
Jean With Elliot & Debbie . . . The Bakers (#3510-01)	151	5
Jean With Elliot . . . The Bakers	159	5
Jennifer With Priscilla . . . The Doll In The Attic	152	1
Jeremiah "Jellybean" Pondhopper	133	4
Jeremy As Noah . . . The Ark Builder	77	2
Jessica And Timmy . . . Animal Hospital	152	2
Jester Q. Funnybones . . . Laugh Often	123	2
Jill . . . Language Of Love	110	2
Jingle Moose	110	3
Jingle Nick	138	3
Jingles & Son With Wreath	110	4
Jingles The Snowman With Wreath	138	4
Jingles With Wreath	145	13
Joy	138	5
Judge Griz . . . Hissonah	63	4
Julia . . . Garden Friends	161	3
Julia With Emmy Lou & Daphne . . . Garden Friends	152	3
Juliette Angel Bear	63	5
Juliette . . . Love Angel	83	1

BEARFINDER – ALPHABETICAL INDEX

	Page #	Pict #
Juliette With Rose	98	13
Justina & M. Harrison . . . Sweetie Pies	64	1
Justina, Bailey & M. Harrison	98	14
Justina Message Bearer	94	2
Justina . . . The Message "Bearer"	64	2
Karen . . . Country Doll	161	4
Karen With Wilson & Eloise . . . Mother's Present (#3515-01)	152	4
Karen With Wilson & Eloise . . . Mother's Present (#3515GCC)	152	5
Katerina & Florence . . . Cold Comfort	130	4
Katherine . . . Kind Hearts	161	5
Katherine With Edmund & Amanda . . . Kind Hearts	153	1
Kelly And Company . . . The Bear Collector	153	2
Kelly The Bear Collector	162	1
Knute & The Gridiron	64	3
Knute . . . Half Time	83	2
Kringle & Bailey With List	64	4
Kringle & Co.	94	3
Kringle And Company (#2283)	64	5
Kringle And Company (#2283-01)	65	1
Kringle & Northrop The Pup	98	15
Kristabell Faeriefrost	130	5
Kristi With Nicole . . . Skater's Waltz	153	3
Krystal Isinglass . . . Snow Angel	111	1
Lady Harriet Rushmore . . . Never Enough Time	123	3
Lady Liberty (#01998-11)	172	1
Lady Liberty (#01998-21)	172	2
Lara . . . Moscow At Midnight	162	2
Larry . . . Nuthin' But Net	83	3
Lars . . . Bells Are Ringing	145	14
Lars . . . Ski, Ski, Ski	139	1
Laura . . . First Day Of School	162	3
Laura With Jane . . . First Day Of School	153	4
Laverne B. Bowler . . . Strikes & Spares	111	2
Lefty On The Mound (#BC2066)	65	3
Lefty On The Mound (#2253)	65	2
Liddy Pearl . . . How Does Your Garden Grow (#2881)	111	3
Liddy Pearl . . . How Does Your Garden Grow (#270602)	143	3
Liddy Pearl . . . They Grow Like Weeds	135	4
Lindsey With Louise . . . The Recital (#3535)	153	5
Lindsey With Louise . . . The Recital (#27551)	158	3
Lizzie . . . The Shopping Angel	111	4
Loretta Moostein . . . "Yer Cheatin' Heart"	111	5
Louella & Hedda . . . The Secret	65	4
Lucinda And Dawn . . . By The Sea (#3536)	154	1
Lucinda And Dawn . . . By The Sea (#27951)	163	3
Lucy Big Pig, Little Pig	65	5
"Lucy" Tigerocious Mommius	168	3
Luminette . . . By The Light Of The Silvery Moon	112	1
Luna . . . By The Light Of The Silvery Moon	112	2
M. Harrison	98	16
M. Harrison . . . The Ambush At Birch Tree	88	1
M. Harrison's Birthday	66	1
Mabel Goodheart . . . Practice Random Acts Of Kindness	98	17
Madge . . . Beautician/Magician	145	15
Madge . . . The Magician/Beautician	112	3
Maisey "The Goil" Grizberg	166	3
Mallory With Patsy & J.B. Bean . . . Trick Or Treat	154	2
Mangianata (Nosh) J. Faeriechild . . . The Cooking Faerie	131	1
Manheim The Eco-Moose	66	2
Manheim The Moose With Wreath	83	4
Margot . . . Dance Dance Dance	98	18
Margot . . . The Ballerina	66	3
Martha Bigheart . . . Love Much	136	1
Mary And Paul . . . The Prayer	154	3
Masterpiece, The	78	4
Matthew . . . As The Drummer	75	1
Matthew With Kip . . . Baby's First Christmas "1997"	83	5
Maynard & Melvin . . . Tales Of The North	88	2
Maynard The Santa Moose	66	4
McDivot . . . Golf, Lie, Golf	145	16
McKenzie . . . Shootin' Star (#25952GCC)	84	1
McKenzie . . . Shootin' Star (#26006)	98	19
Megan With Elliot & Annie . . . Christmas Carol	154	4
Megan With Elliot . . . Christmas Carol (#2720)	164	1
Megan With Elliot . . . Christmas Carol (#25850)	160	1
"Mel" Otterrificus	169	1
Melissa . . . The Ballet	162	4
Melissa With Katie . . . The Ballet	154	5
Melvin . . . The Jingle Moose	145	17
Mercy . . . Angel Of Nurses	112	4
Meredith With Jacqueline . . . Daisy Chain	155	1
Michelle With Daisy . . . Reading Is Fun	155	2
Miles "Gobble" Grizberg	166	4
Miliken Von Hinden Moose . . . Tree's Company	113	1
Milo . . . Up, Up, And Away	98	20
Minerva . . . The Baseball Angel	113	2
Minerva With Daffodils	145	18
Minerva's Flight	145	19
Miss Bruin & Bailey	94	4
Miss Prudence . . . Multiplication	113	3
Mistletoe & Holly – First Christmas "1997"	139	2
Mistress Bailey	99	1
Momma . . . Anticipation	99	2
Momma Grizberg . . . Egg Decorator	166	5
Momma McBear & Caledonia . . . Quiet Time	66	5
Momma McBear . . . Anticipation	67	1
Montague Von Hindenmoose . . . Surprise!	113	4
Moriarty – The Bear In The Cat Suit	67	2
Ms. Ashley . . . The Teacher	162	5
Ms. Berriweather's Cottage	172	3
Ms. Bruin & Bailey . . . Tea Time	88	3
Ms. Bruin & Bailey . . . The Lesson (#2259)	67	3
Ms. Bruin & Bailey . . . The Lesson (#270554)	80	2
Ms. Bruin . . . As The Teacher	75	2
Ms. Bruin . . . Learn!	99	3
Ms. Fries . . . Guardian Angel Of Waitresses	113	5
Ms. Fries . . . Not Quite The Guardian Angel Of Waitresses	113	5
Ms. Griz . . . Monday Morning	67	4
Ms. Griz . . . Saturday Night	67	5
Ms. Imin Payne . . . NQGA Of Exercisers	114	1
Ms. Lilypond . . . Lesson #1	133	5
Ms. McFrazzle . . . Care Giver	145	20
Ms. McFrazzle . . . Daycare Extraordinaire	114	2
Ms. Patience . . . Angel Of Teachers	114	3
Ms. Patience . . . Teach, Learn	146	2
Ms. Patience . . . The Teacher	146	1
Ms. Prudence . . . Teach, Learn	146	3
Murgatroyd The Chrismoose	99	4
Myron R. Fishmeister . . . Angel Of Fish Stories	114	4
Myrtle . . . Believe!	115	1
Nana & Aubergine & Peapod	146	4

	Page #	Pict #
Nana McHare . . . And The Love Gardeners	115	2
Na-Nick And Siegfried . . . The Plan	115	3
Na-Nick Of The North (#2650)	146	5
Na-Nick Of The North (#2804)	115	4
Nanny . . . The Snowmom	115	5
Nanuk . . . Winter Wonderland	139	3
Natalie With Joy . . . Sunday School	155	3
Neville . . . As Joseph	75	3
Neville Bedtime	94	5
Neville . . . Compubear	68	1
Neville Compubear	95	1
Neville . . . The Bedtime Bear	68	2
Nicholai . . . With Dove	146	6
Nicholai With Tree (#2550)	139	4
Nicholai With Tree (#2800)	116	1
Nicholai With Tree (#26300)	146	7
Nicholas	99	5
Nicholas The Giftgiver	139	5
Nicholas "Uncle Nick" Grizberg	167	1
Nicholas With Book Of Lists	116	2
Nicholas . . . With Tree	146	8
Nick On Ice	125	3
Nicknoah . . . Santa With Ark	116	3
Niki With Candle	116	4
Noah . . . And The Golden Rule	88	4
Noah & Co	90	3
Noah & Co . . . Ark Builders	68	3
Noah's Genius At Work Table	172	4
Noel Bruinski . . Da Electrician "1998"	84	9
Nome Sweet Home	146	9
No-No-Nick . . . Bad Boy Santa	116	5
Northbound Willie	117	1
"Nosh" . . . What's Cooking?!?!	146	10
Oceania	146	11
Oceania . . . Ocean Angel	117	2
Olaf . . . I Luuv Snow	146	12
Olaf . . . Let It Snow (#2560)	140	1
Olaf . . . Let It Snow (#25650)	140	2
Olaf . . . Mogul Meister	117	3
Olaf . . . The Flakey Snowman	146	13
Olivia . . . Wishing You "Peace"	140	3
Otis . . . Tax Time	68	4
Otis . . . The Fisherman	68	5
P.J. McSnoozin With Craxton . . . Hibearnation	117	4
Patricia With Molly . . . Attic Treasures	155	4
Peacenik . . . The Sixties Santa	117	5
Peacenik Santa	146	14
Pearl . . . The Knitter	131	2
Pearl Too . . . The Knitter	131	3
Peter . . . The Whopper	118	1
Plant With Hope, Grow With Love, Bloom With Joy	172	5
Polaris And The North Star . . . On Ice	118	2
Prince Hamalot	69	1
Prudence . . . Daffodils	118	3
Prudence Mooselmaid . . . The Pilgrim	118	4
Puck . . . Slapshot	69	2
Puff & Nessie Lochlegend	169	3
Puff Lochlegend	169	2
Punkin Puss	99	6
Purrscilla & Friends	146	15
Purrscilla G. Pussenboots . . . Mitten Knitters	118	5
Purrscilla . . . Give Thanks	119	1
Queen, The	99	7
Queen Bee	99	8
Rachael, Barbara & Matthew . . . Sabbath Lights	155	5
Raeburn	173	1
Raleigh . . . As Balthasar	75	4
Ralph Angel Pooch	146	16
"Ray" Croccodiopius	169	4
Rebecca With Elliot . . . Birthday	156	1
Regina D. Ferrisdaval . . . I Am The Queen	84	3
Remembrance Angelflyte . . . Time Flies	131	4
Robin . . . Peace On Earth	140	4
Robin . . . The Snowbird Lover	119	2
Rocky . . . All Star	79	2
Rocky Bruin . . . Score, Score, Score	69	3
Rocky . . . Goal Kick	99	9
Rocky . . . Score, Score, Score	84	4
Rose . . . Garden Classics	99	10
Rufus . . . Hoe Down	119	3
Ryan & Diane . . . Love Is Forever	164	2
S.C. Northstar & Emmett . . . Lil' Helper	69	4
S.C. Northstar . . . Ho! Ho! Ho!	99	11
S.C. Ribbit . . . Hoppy Christmas	134	1
S.S. Noah . . . The Ark	77	3
St. Nick . . . The Quest	119	4
Sabrina . . . Bippity Boppity Boo!	146	17
Salem . . . Give Thanks	119	5
Sandra Claus . . . Christmas Morning	156	2
Sandra S. Claus	156	4
Santa . . . And The Final Inspection (#370003)	123	4
Santa . . . And The Final Inspection (#370203)	140	5
Santa . . . And The Final Inspection (#370503)	146	18
Santa Cat	99	12
Santa . . . In The Nick Of Time (#370000)	124	1
Santa . . . In The Nick Of Time (#370200)	141	1
Santa . . . In The Nick Of Time (#370500)	146	19
Santa Jr . . . And The Final Inspection	123	5
Santa Jr . . . In The Nick Of Time	124	2
Santa Jr . . . Quick As A Flash	124	4
Santa . . . Quick As A Flash (#370004)	124	3
Santa . . . Quick As A Flash (#370204)	141	2
Santa . . . Quick As A Flash (#370504)	146	20
Santa's Challenge	125	4
Santa's Flight Plan (#2703)	143	4
Santa's Flight Plan (#3000)	126	1
Santa's Frame Shop	136	2
Santa's Hobby . . . The Teddy Bear Maker	126	2
Santoad	147	1
Sarah & Heather With Elliot, Dolly & Amelia . . . Tea For Four	156	3
Sebastian And Nicholas . . . The Lost Ball	88	5
Sebastian's Prayer	69	5
Secret, The	95	2
Seraphina With Jacob & Rachael . . . The Choir Angels	120	1
Serena . . . Joy Angel	84	5
Serendipity . . . As The Guardian Angel	75	5
Serendipity . . . "Peace" To All	85	1
Serenity . . . The Mother's Angel	120	2
Sgt. Bookum O'Reilly . . . To Protect & Serve	167	2
Sgt. Rex & Matt . . . The Runaway	120	3
Shannon & Wilson . . . Wait'n For Grandma	156	4
Shelby . . . Asleep In Teddy's Arms	157	1
Shelby Turtlecrawlius	169	5
Shelley's Flight	99	13
Sherlock & Watson . . . In Disguise	70	1
Siegfried & Egon . . . The Sign	120	4
Siegfried The Santa Moose	147	2
Simone & Bailey	95	3
Simone & Bailey . . . Helping Hands (#2267)	70	2
Simone & Bailey . . . Helping Hands (#2705)	90	4
Simone de Bearvoire & Her Mom, My Auntie Alice	70	3
Simone In Heart Wreath	99	14
Sir Edmund . . . Persistence	70	4
Sir Simon Steadfast . . . Always Enough Time	124	5

	Page #	Pict #
Sliknick In The Chimney	141	3
Sliknick On The Chimney	147	3
Sliknick . . . The Chimney Sweep	120	5
Slurp . . . 5¢ A Lick	147	4
Slurp And The Snowcone Stand	131	5
"Smiley" Hippotoothocus	170	1
Snowbeary & The Snowflakes	99	15
Snowy . . . The First Sign Of Spring	99	16
Sparky And The Box	70	5
Sparky McPlug	121	1
"Speedy" . . . Fast As I Can!	147	5
Spitz And Floyd Frogswimium . . . Easy Method Swim School	170	2
Springtime Bessie	99	17
Stage . . . School Pageant, The	76	1
Stanley The Stick Handler	132	1
Starry Starry Night	141	4
Stella . . . Believe In Angels	99	18
Stephanie With Jim . . . School Days	157	2
Stonewall . . . The Rebel	71	1
Stretch & Skye . . . The Lookouts	77	4
Sunny And Sally Berriweather . . . Plant With Hope	173	2
T.H. Bean . . . The Bearmaker Elf	132	2
T.H.B. & Co . . . Work Is Love Made Visible	71	3
Ted & Teddy (#2223)	71	2
Ted & Teddy (#2701SF)	95	4
Teresa And John . . . The Prayer	157	4
Thaddeus "Bud" Grizberg	167	3
Thatcher & Eden . . . As The Camel	76	2
Theresa & John . . . The Prayer	163	2
Theresa . . . As Mary	76	3
"Think" Library Book	142	2
Tiffany . . . "Forever"	158	4
Too Loose Lapin	147	6
"Too Loose" Lapin . . . "The Arte-e-st"	121	2
Tulip . . . An Armful Of Blooms	99	19
TuTu C. Ribbit . . . Frog Lake	134	2
Tuxworth P. Cummerbund	132	3
'Twas The Night Before Christmas	79	1
Uncle Elliot	173	3
Uncle Elliot . . . The Head Bean Wants You	173	4
Uncle Gus & Gary . . . The Gift	71	4
Uncle Irving Grizberg	167	4
Union Jack . . . Love Letters	71	5
Velma Q. Berriweather	173	5
Velma Q. Berriweather . . . The Cookie Queen	173	1
Victoria . . . City Doll	163	1
Victoria Regina Buzzbruin . . . So Many Flowers, So Little Time	72	1
Victoria . . . The Lady	72	2

	Page #	Pict #
Victoria With Samantha . . . Victorian Ladies	157	4
Virginia "Ginny" Grizberg	167	5
Walter T. Goodlife . . . Live Well	125	1
Wanda & Gert . . . A Little Off The Top	72	3
Wendy . . . Wash Day	163	2
Wendy Willowhare . . . A Tisket A Tasket	121	3
Wendy With Bronte, Keats, Tennyson & Poe . . . Wash Day (#3521)	158	1
Wendy With Bronte, Keats, Tennyson And Poe . . . Wash Day (#2711SF)	164	5
Whitney With Wilson . . . Tea And Candlelight	163	5
Whitney With Wilson . . . Tea Party (#3523)	158	2
Whitney With Wilson . . . Tea Party (#272001)	159	3
Willie With Broom	141	5
Willie With Evergreens	147	7
Wilson . . . As Melchior	76	4
Wilson At The Beach	72	4
Wilson . . . Hugs & Kisses	99	20
Wilson . . . In Love	100	1
Wilson . . . Life Is But A Dream	79	3
Wilson The Perfesser	72	5
Wilson The Wizard . . . Boo!	100	2
Wilson . . . The Wonderful Wizard Of Wuz	73	1
Wilson With Love Sonnets (#2007)	73	2
Wilson With Love Sonnets (#2750SF)	95	4
Wilson With Love Sonnets (#26020)	100	3
Wilson With Shooting Star	85	2
Wilson's Flight	100	4
Windy The Snowman	147	8
Windy With Book	121	4
Windy With Tree	142	1
Wings To Soar	79	4
Winkie & Dink . . . As The Lambs	76	5
Winnie Hopkins & Bunnylove	168	1
Yukon, Kodiak & Nanuk . . . Nome Sweet Home	143	5
Yukon & Kodiak . . . Nome Sweet Home	143	1
"Zeb" Bearimonius Poppius	170	3
Zelma G. Berriweather	174	2
Ziggy . . . The Duffer	121	5
Zoe . . . Starlight Christmas	85	3
Zoe . . . The Angel Of Life	73	3

ACKNOWLEDGEMENTS

CheckerBee Publishing would like to extend a special thanks to Harry & Millie Croft (*Palatine, IL*) and Suzie Hocker (*Morton, IL*). Also thanks to Linda Brand, Julie Christensen, Brenda Fry, Teddy Huppert, Ed & Janet Hymes, Sally Jechura, Shari Martin, Annmarie Pearlstein, Dave & Linda Reinhart, Mark & Jean Ann Sovereign, Linda Stratton, Diana Webb and Linda Wise, and all the Boyds collectors and retailers who contributed their valuable time to assist us with this book. Many thanks to the great people at The Boyds Collection Ltd.

Ty® Beanie
Babies®

Ty® Plush
Animals

BOYDS BEARS & FRIENDS™

The
BOYDS COLLECTION LTD.

Charming Tails

Cherished
Teddies®
by ENESCO®

Department 56®
Snowbabies™

Department 56®
Villages

Dreamsicles®

HALLMARK
Keepsake Ornaments

HARBOUR
LIGHTS®

Precious
Moments®
by ENESCO

SWAROVSKI
Silver Crystal

Boyds Bears & Friends™
presents the

1999 F.o.B. Membership

Plant with Hope...Grow with Love...Bloom with Joy!

The Loyal Order of Friends of Boyds™

This is it!
This is how you become a
Genuine "Bloomin' F.o.B.!"

That's an Official 1999 Member of...

The Loyal Order of Friends of Boyds™

(F.o.Bs for Short!)

A Slightly Off-Center Collector's Club
for people who still believe in...
BEARS AND HARES YOU CAN TRUST™

And have we got a story for you, turn the page ☞

Here it iz...yer very own, extra special Membership Application!

And you don't have to wait until your anniversary date
(the date you joined the Club) to renew!

CHECK ONE: ❑ Current Member ID# _____
❑ New Member

NAME _____

ADDRESS _____

CITY _____

STATE _____ZIP CODE _____

DAYTIME PHONE (_____) _____

DATE OF BIRTH *(year optional)* _____

❑ YES, I want to be a "Bloomin' F.o.B." for $32.^{50}
(PA residents with 6% sales tax = $34.45)

❑ Make it a 2-Year Membership instead
(Good thru 2000!), just **$63.00** _____
(PA residents with 6% sales tax = $66.78)

❑ Add The Official F.o.B. Mug $7.^{50}
(PA residents with 6% sales tax = $7.95)

GRAND TOTAL _____

FORM OF PAYMENT: ❑ Check ❑ Money Order

MAKE PAYABLE TO: The Boyds Collection Ltd.®
P.O. Box 4386 F.o.B. Dept.
Gettysburg, PA 17325-4386

CREDIT CARD CHOICE: ❑ Master Card ❑ Visa

CREDIT CARD NUMBER: Exp. Date ___/___/___

AUTHORIZED SIGNATURE:

_____

*(Authorized signature must accompany charge request.
Card will be processed at time of shipment.)*
I understand that my membership kit will be shipped 12 to 16 weeks
following receipt of this application at The Boyds Collection.
Offer Expires December 31, 1999

WHO IS YOUR RETAILER?
(you know the place where you purchase your Boyds stuff)

Name _____ ID# _____

City _____ State ____ Zip _____

Once upon a time in the Land of Boyds...

...lived Flora Mae Berriweather and her daughter Blossum. Flora was famous for her Green Thumb...she seemed to win all of the Blue Ribbons in Gardening at the County Fair. Blossum wanted to plant a garden and be just like her Mom!

🐾 One day Flora Mae said, "Blossum, I have some special seeds for your Garden." And she told Blossum the secrets of growing a good garden. She said, "If you think you <u>can</u> do something, you <u>will</u> be able to do it. So remember...**Plant with Hope**, (the first secret) and see what happens!"

🐾 So Blossum found a sunny spot for planting...and soon a green shoot appeared. Every day she applied the second secret...watered it & talked to it, and her little plant **Grew with Love**...and *grew*, and GREW into a Giant Sunflower twice as tall as Blossum herself! Flora Mae proudly watched her daughter, and one summer day she said, "Blossum, get your Sunflower ready for the judging at tomorrow's County Fair!"

🐾 Well, when ol' Judge Griz (who moonlights as a County Fair Judge, you know) came to Blossum's Sunflower, he saw right away that it deserved the Blue Ribbon...and the only thing bigger & brighter than that bloomin' Sunflower was the smile on Blossum's face as she learned the final secret...**Bloom with Joy!**

♦♦♦

So, to remind you to "**Plant with Hope...Grow with Love...Bloom with Joy!**", in <u>anything</u> you do...here's our 1999 Club Kit. Reward or encourage yourself or a Special Someone with our "Blossum" and "Flora Mae" pieces!

🐾 **Flora Mae Berriweather...Grow with Love!** She's a Bee-you-ti-ful 6" bear dressed in a buttercup yellow handknit cardigan sweater & matching sunny yellow felt hat complete with a big ol' Sunflower on the front. (Aunt Mabel, eat your heart out!)

🐾 **"Blossum B. Berriweather... Bloom with Joy!"** Exclusive Bearstone This one's a dandy! Blossum is standing under her prize winning sunflower which has grown to a whopping 4¼" high (well, that's a <u>Giant</u> in Boyds Bearstone Land!)

🐾 Genuine "**Bloomin' F.o.B.**" Sunflower Seed Packet! This is sooo luverly, if we do say so ourselves. The custom-designed Sunflower Seed Packet is 'specially created only for "Bloomin' F.o.B.s." And yes, there really <u>are</u> genuine Sunflower seeds in there!

🐾 **A Year's Subscription to the F.o.B. Inquirer -** The only newspaper written by The Head Bean Hisself! And guess what? In response to Popular Demand by our current F.o.B.s (see...we do listen!) we will Double our number of Issues. Okay...that means we're going from 2 issues per year to 4 - but that's as fast as The Head Bean can write!

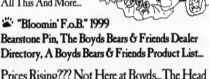

All This And More...

🐾 "**Bloomin' F.o.B.**" 1999 Bearstone Pin, The Boyds Bears & Friends Dealer Directory, A Boyds Bears & Friends Product List...

Prices Rising??? Not Here at Boyds...The Head Bean says Membership is **Still Only $32.50!**

♦♦♦

But Wait! We're slaving away to bring you Extra Special Opportunities too...and they're available only to our 1999 Club Members!

First...The chance to buy the new first-ever **1999 Official F.o.B. Mug!** Yep! That's Right! This exclusive Members Only Piece features some of the custom artwork of the seed packet (and more!) wrapped around a luverly mug. And it's a lot neater than trying to drink your coffee from that seed packet to proclaim you're a "Bloomin' F.o.B."!

Second...our exclusive Members Only Plush Bears, **Hope, Love and Joy** and our Bearstone piece, **Sunny and Sally**...that you can order from your favorite B.B. & F. Retailer...this year!